Testimonials

'Rare is the leader who not only walks the talk but also gracefully and courageously exemplifies authenticity and vulnerability and shares the story for others to learn from. Julia Gibney's 'Break Free' is that story – a must-read for women in STEM and anyone seeking a fresh perspective on professional authenticity. Gibney seamlessly weaves personal anecdotes, insightful stories, and research to illuminate the transformative power of staying true to oneself in a world that often discourages it. She navigates the unique challenges women face in male-dominated industries, combining humour and wisdom to illustrate the superpower of embracing authenticity.'

– Lea Vesic, Director, Aviation Academy, RMIT University

'A compelling read, filled with honest insights on finding and achieving one's purpose. Julia has used her experience and successes to describe her lifelong journey towards authenticity. In so doing, she has created a fantastic resource for those in the early stages of their careers as well as those at later career stages, interested in change, transformation and continuous development.'

– Kristen Raby, Acting General Manager, Major Service Provider – Strategic Workforce Planning, Nova Systems

Break Free!

Break Free!

Activate Your Authenticity
Embrace a Journey of Self-Discovery

JULIA GIBNEY

Break Free! Activate Your Authenticity: Embrace a Journey of Self-Discovery

For author queries or further information, visit www.winterandassociates.com.au

Cover image by Vecteezy
Text and cover design by BookPOD
Editing by Renée Otmar reneeotmar.com.au
Printed by Ingram Spark

ISBN: 978-0-6459980-0-9 (pbk) 978-0-6459980-1-6 (e-book)

NATIONAL LIBRARY OF AUSTRALIA

A catalogue record for this book is available from the National Library of Australia

Important Notice Regarding Health and Counselling Advice

This book is designed to assist the reader with strategies to find meaning in their lives. It aims to promote the benefits of coaching and mentoring.

Coaching emphasises a forward-looking approach in facilitating development and growth through short-term, medium-term and long-term objectives, and achievable goals. Working with a coach or mentor who employs illuminating and perceptive questioning methods can assist in devising strategies for success. Coaching and mentoring can support progress towards clearly defined objectives.

However, it is important to note that coaching and mentoring should not be confused with therapy or counselling. While therapy delves into the past and addresses aspects of an individual's life that could benefit from the expertise of a psychologist, coaching maintains a future-oriented perspective, concentrating on transformative techniques that yield positive outcomes.

Readers seeking therapy or counselling are advised to seek guidance from suitably qualified health practitioners or counsellors.

Every person's situation is distinct, and what works for one person may not be suitable for another. Health-related matters, emotional wellbeing and personal concerns require personalised attention and professional expertise.

The insights offered in this book are intended to complement, not replace, the expertise of qualified mental health professionals who can assess your specific needs and provide tailored guidance. While the information presented within these pages is meant to be informative and thought-provoking, it should never replace personalised advice from a professional who has a deep understanding of your unique circumstances.

Readers are urged to consult with a licensed health practitioner or counsellor before making any significant decisions or implementing changes based on the content of this book. Seeking professional advice is an essential step in making informed choices that are best suited to individual circumstances.

This book is lovingly dedicated to my two remarkable daughters, Melanie and Kimberley. Their patience and understanding during my journey of self-discovery and growth as a parent have been a constant source of inspiration. I am grateful for their presence in my life, as they have taught me valuable lessons about love, resilience and the power of family.

I extend my heartfelt gratitude to my wonderful husband, Rob. His unwavering support, encouragement and acceptance of who I truly am have been instrumental in my personal and professional development.

Rob, Melanie and Kimberley, you are the foundation of my happiness and the driving force behind my aspirations. Your love and belief in me have propelled me forward, enabling me to embrace authenticity and pursue my dreams. I am forever grateful for your presence and steadfast support.

Contents

Preface

As I begin to share the thoughts and insights captured within these pages, I am prompted to reflect on the diverse avenues that have intertwined to give rise to this book. Its genesis arose in those moments when several of my mentees expressed an interest in the source of my passion and drive. The book emerged from a sincere curiosity, nurtured by my professional practice in engineering, coaching and mentoring, and my interest in the study of psychology and human behaviour.

Countless conversations and interactions I have had the privilege to engage in throughout my journey provided the motivation to write the book. From the corridors of academia to the dynamic landscapes of my professional life, I have found myself constantly drawn to understanding the intricacies of human behaviour and the ways in which our experiences shape us.

The ideas of this book are offered, not as definitive answers, but as considerations for you to ponder and explore. The scenarios I present within these pages are inspired by real events, although their details have been blended and reshaped to protect the identities of those involved. My intention is to offer practical insights while respecting the confidentiality of the people who have entrusted me with their stories.

This book is crafted to illuminate your path of self-discovery and introspection. It might helpfully serve as a companion on your transformative journey towards heightened self-awareness, confidence and fulfilment. As you navigate its pages, you are invited to unveil the profound rewards that come with embracing authenticity – from forging deeper connections with others to cultivating a heightened sense of self-awareness.

I recommend that you approach this book as a source of inspiration, reflection and practical insight. It is my hope that you will find value in the ideas presented here, whether you are an engineer seeking to understand the human side of technology or simply interested in exploring the fascinating interplay between psychology and professional development.

Thank you for joining me in this exploration. Your decision to embark on this intellectual adventure means a great deal to me, and I am excited to share these insights with you.

Warm regards,

Julia Gibney

Introduction

Embarking on the journey of this book, you will find that its contents have been shaped by my professional experience and the unique path that has brought me to this work. As you engage with the ideas in the ensuing chapters, you will encounter fragments of my personal narrative, interwoven with insights and strategies for reflection on your own approach. While you may wish to read from beginning to end, consider this book an open invitation to explore the chapters on the basis of your own interests. Chapter 1 sets out a solid foundation for understanding why authenticity is important, so I recommend that you start there and then freely delve into other parts of the book that pique your interest. Aspects of my own story are revealed throughout as they harmonise with the broader themes of the book. The objective is to provide a versatile toolkit that can be aligned with your personal journey, offering both guidance and empowerment along the way.

How I got to here

On a warm spring morning in Sydney, I found myself standing on the steps of the Australian Defence Force Recruiting Centre, which is nestled on bustling Liverpool Street. I arrived a staggering 25 minutes ahead of schedule, anxiously anticipating the commencement of my first round of aptitude testing to join the Royal Australian Navy. My mind was a whirlwind of doubts and uncertainties, my trembling hands betraying the unease within.

"What on earth am I doing here?" I muttered to myself, the words barely audible over the thumping of my racing heart. My thoughts continued, "I don't think I am up for this. I didn't finish high school... I left home at 15, I have no life experience, what could I even offer them?"

This chorus of self-doubt reverberated, each note playing a symphony of inadequacy through my thought process. The imposter syndrome, a relentless companion, often takes such opportune moments to surface, drowning out any flicker of confidence. The thought of escape danced across my consciousness, tempting me with the allure of plausible excuses to present to my husband, should I decide to abandon this nerve-wracking endeavour. I realised that I was surrounded by others, each dealing with their own anxieties. Some people were accompanied by parents, encouraging and urging them forward on this uncertain journey. Thoughts of what my father might say emerged, but I quickly dismissed them. Dad's critical responses always cast a shadow over my accomplishments. Nothing I did ever seemed to measure up to his expectations, and it was no surprise that self-doubt was enveloping me like a suffocating fog. Yet, in that pivotal moment, I decided that it was now or never, summoning the courage to climb the steps to the entrance of the Recruiting Centre.

In the lift to the 10th floor, my palms moist with sweat, and I stole glances at other prospective recruits, hoping to blend into the background. About 20 young people, wearing expressions mirroring my own trepidation, clutched folders filled with resumes, school reports, letters of recommendation and other documents.

Approaching the counter, in an attempt to sound confident, I stated my purpose, which was to sit the aptitude test that would give me a chance to join the Navy. The Leading Seaman enquired after my name and collected the necessary documentation, leaving me to join the others in the waiting room. There was a heavy hush in the air as we avoided each other's gazes, imprisoned by our collective fear. Eventually, we were summoned into a large room, where instructions on the day's proceedings were explained.

First would come general numeracy and literacy tests, followed by aptitude assessments to probe our reasoning and problem-solving abilities. After lunch, those of us who met the stringent standards of these tests would be examined by a psychologist, who would assess our mental and emotional suitability.

To my surprise and delight, I persevered in test after test, advancing through the rounds without fail. Lunch offered a brief reprieve from the tension that hung around like an invisible cloak.

After lunch we were segregated into two groups: those suitable and those deemed unsuitable. I was fortunate to be deemed suitable, a small victory among the many uncertainties. By afternoon, the time came to explore the roles that aligned with my capabilities. We were told to wait, the minutes stretching into what felt like aeons, until finally, I was called into yet another room, where I receive the unexpected news that my test results were exceptional. I was offered the opportunity to become an avionics technician, a role previously unbeknown to me. The recruiter explained that it was akin to an electronics technician, but specifically for aircraft. I found the very idea captivating, and without consideration or further questioning, I accepted the offer, selecting a few alternative roles as backups, just in case they got it wrong.

By late afternoon I emerged from the building, triumphant, but also mentally and physically drained. The testing was exhausting and I was filled with a whirlwind of emotions. As I walked to Central Station, a newfound lightness permeated my being. I was excited and could not wait to share the news with my husband. I relished the chance to tell him that I had been offered one of the most challenging roles in the Navy – as a woman, no less! Little did I know, as an 18-year-old, the true extent of what lay ahead.

Fast-forward 18 months to Valentine's Day in 1994, and once again I found myself standing on the familiar steps of that same building. This time I was newly separated from my husband, unburdened by ties that once held me in Sydney. I ascended those steps with a mix of curiosity and apprehension, knowing that this journey would likely be anything but ordinary. Thoughts swirled through my mind. Among them was a recognition that I was about to make a solemn declaration, pledging my allegiance to Queen Elizabeth II and vowing to serve and protect my country in the Royal Australian Navy for at least the following six years.

Leaping further ahead in time, 23 years almost to the day, I exited the doors of Defence Plaza in Melbourne. In the years following my graduation, I experienced two dysfunctional marriages and became a single parent to two beautiful girls. Along the way, I acquired an engineering degree, not one but two masters' degrees, and a lifetime's worth of experiences. There was just one element missing from my life journey and career – the sea time I signed up for when I graduated, which would have given me the opportunity to travel the world and embark on grand adventures. Thus, the story was far from over.

In the years following my departure from the Navy, I embarked on a meandering path through a series of jobs, finding myself grappling with an unrelenting imposter syndrome. Despite the polished facade I presented to the world, I continued to conceal my true struggles, so much so it became an art form. I was accustomed to wearing an array of "masks", each one obscuring my authentic self. The result was a gradual erosion of both my sense of identity and any genuine aspirations I may once have nurtured.

I became skilled at appeasing others, diligently adhering to well-intentioned advice when it came from people I admired. Yes sometimes I was defiant, rebelling against suggestions, just to prove a point to those whose opinions I did not agree with. However, in this intricate dance of people-pleasing, I did not pause to consider my own needs and desires. Outwardly, I projected an image of confidence, success and sociability, a masterful performance that masked the truth: a cavernous emptiness within. Anxiety, self-loathing and erratic mood swings became my unwelcome companions behind closed doors, where I lived with the silent symphony of my hidden turmoil.

What finally brought an end to this cycle of turmoil? The answer lies within the pages that follow, which are a testament to the long and arduous journey I have endured. Surprisingly, midway through my military career I had a rude awakening, precipitated by one of the few people I truly admired. It made me stop and take stock of what I really wanted. My transformation had begun.

Amidst my hollow achievements came a pivotal moment of reckoning. It demanded my undivided attention, urging me to pause and reflect upon the path I had taken. During this introspective interlude, the seeds of purpose within me began to sprout, beckoning me towards a more meaningful existence. Like an acorn maturing into a majestic oak tree, I gradually experienced my own maturing and personal growth, year after year. Just as trees weather great storms, for me some years were more challenging than others. And just as mighty storms can batter and bruise, I too found myself tested and worn from the relentless ebb and flow of life's tempestuous winds, which threatened to uproot me from my core.

But always, there lay within me the potential for transformation. Like the resilient trees that withstand the harshest gales, I discovered an inherent strength. Life may have left me feeling battered and bruised, but it also forged my resilience and deepened my resolve. I learned valuable lessons about perseverance, adaptability and the indomitable spirit within.

The winds of life may have shaken me to my core, but they did not break me. Rather, they propelled me towards a greater sense of self-awareness and inner strength. Over time I became grounded and rooted in my true essence. Each gust of adversity revealed my capacity for resilience and the untapped potential that lay dormant within. I emerged stronger and wiser, and ready to face the challenges that lay ahead.

The transformation was steady and continuous. I allowed myself to linger in moments of contemplation, earnestly assessing the tapestry of my life. In exploring the reasons for my choices, I delved beyond the surface to understand the intricate motivations that guided my actions. And in those sacred moments of unabashed self-reflection, a deep realisation washed over me, and an imperative truth took hold. If I truly desired authentic happiness, if I yearned to embrace the boundless potential that lay dormant within me, then change was no longer a luxury but a necessity. It was time to shed the layers of pretence, to discard the facades that confined me, and to embark on a transformative journey towards becoming the most radiant manifestation of my own being.

That is the basis of my story.

Dear Reader, join me as I uncover my own transformative expedition. This was a process that spanned many years, requiring from me introspection, courage and a steadfast commitment to self-discovery. Throughout the pages ahead, I share the invaluable lessons I have learned along the way, the pivotal moments that shaped my understanding of authenticity, and the methods that helped me to break free from the chains that bound me.

The path to self-awareness is a winding one, filled with twists and turns, triumphs and setbacks. In this book I seek to help you navigate the maze of self-doubt and confusion that accompanies us all. Empower yourself to emerge transformed and whole, armed with the tools needed to shed your masks, embrace your true self and live a life defined by purpose and fulfilment.

1

The Importance of Authenticity

What is authenticity?

Authenticity is usually defined as the truth or veracity of something. In recent times it has also come to be popularly described as a virtue. But being authentic is more than a buzzword; it is an insightful way of living that holds the key to finding genuine fulfilment, happiness and success. In a world that often urges us to conform, embracing authenticity can be a powerful tool in crafting a meaningful life that resonates with our true essence.

At its core, authenticity is about being true to ourselves, cherishing our unique qualities and living in harmony with our deepest values and beliefs. It involves cultivating transparency in our thoughts, feelings and intentions, and aligning our actions with our authentic selves. Although the idea of living authentically may seem straightforward, it can be both challenging and rewarding.

This chapter discusses the significance of authenticity, exploring how seeking to live authentically can enrich our lives and lead us to great self-discovery and growth. In the following pages ahead, we uncover the essence of living authentically and discover the profound effect it can have on our wellbeing and overall sense of purpose.

The price of not living authentically

For 23 years, I prioritised the needs of others, conformed to societal expectations of being a wife, mother, daughter and naval officer, without questioning why I was living that way or considering the damage I was doing to my relationship with my children, my (former) husband and, most importantly, with myself.

In the pursuit of what others deemed to be my full potential, I was often consumed with anxiety. Nights became restless, requiring medication to find solace in sleep. I yearned for tranquillity as I closed my eyes, only to be haunted by recurring nightmares that were fuelled by unsettling "what if" scenarios. The situation reached a tipping point when my lack of authenticity began to pose a threat to my military career. To move forward, I had to confront my self-sabotaging tendencies head-on.

The incessant thoughts that invaded my early mornings and kept me wide awake at night demanded my attention. It was essential for my wellbeing that I break free from the shackles of living up to someone else's expectations. I needed to discover who I truly was and align my actions with my own values and aspirations. It was no longer acceptable for me to conform to the standards prescribed by others; it was time to live on my own terms.

In today's society, we are often bombarded with messages and expectations of others about who we should be and how we should live our lives. We may be told that we need to conform to societal norms or follow a certain path in order to be successful or happy. As a result, many of us find ourselves living lives that do not align with our true selves or hiding parts of ourselves in order to fit in or please others.

I can definitely relate to this. I undertook an education path that I really did not want to, in pursuit of an idea about being better, smarter and more likeable, so that I might please a bunch of people who really did not care how I truly felt or what I really thought. As long as I portrayed an image of invulnerability and success, and lived up to the reputation of being a successful, career-driven woman, it would maintain the status quo. And the more I did it, the more I hated myself for doing it, and the more damage it did to my relationship with my children.

This kind of fake living can be exhausting and unfulfilling in the long run. When we stray from our true selves, we experience a disconnection, feelings of discontent and even despair. It feels as though we are not reaching our full potential or living a life that aligns with who we truly are. However, there is an empowering solution: authenticity.

The rewards of living authentically

By wholeheartedly embracing our genuine selves and living in accordance with our core values and beliefs, we pave the way for a life that is uniquely ours. This choice holds the key to unlocking greater happiness, fulfillment and success, both in our personal lives and in our professional endeavours.

Living authentically can also provoke a transformative journey of self-discovery and growth. By embracing our true selves, we uncover parts of ourselves that we never knew existed, or tap into strengths and talents that we may have been hiding. We may also find that our relationships become deeper and more meaningful, as we are able to connect at a more authentic level.

Of course, embracing authenticity is not always easy. It demands vulnerability, taking risks and letting go of what no longer serves us. It requires us to confront and conquer our fears, insecurities and limiting beliefs that have hindered our progress. At times, embracing authenticity can feel like a dance in which we take two steps forward and one step back. The allure of sticking with the status quo, and avoiding making waves, can be tempting; it can result in regression when we should be forging ahead.

Undeniably, the journey to living authentically can be arduous. It demands from us unwavering effort, and not everyone is willing or able to embark on such a transformative path. In my personal life, I have faced moments of overwhelming frustration, where surrender seemed like the easiest option. Yet, in those moments, by challenging my own thinking I was opening myself to authenticity. I embraced the power of taking small steps, each one bolder and more assured than the last, not unlike a mountain goat seeking to navigate a rocky ledge. Through rugged determination, I steadily progressed, learning never to underestimate the significance of each stride forward.

The rewards of living authentically are well worth the effort. By embracing our true selves and living in a way that is authentic and aligned with our core values and beliefs, we can create a life that is truly our own, and find happiness, fulfillment and success in the process.

Why authenticity matters

In a world that often values conformity, why is it important to embrace our true selves and live authentically? First and foremost, authenticity enables us to connect more deeply with ourselves. When we live out of alignment, we may find ourselves disconnected from our true desires, passions and values. We may feel like we are "going through the motions" in life, without a true sense of purpose or direction. But when we embrace our true reality, we can connect deeply with our inner selves and tap into purpose and meaning that come from living in alignment with our values.

As society inundates us with unrealistic ideals and stereotypes through news and social media, the urgency to embrace genuineness becomes more pronounced. In our swiftly evolving world, the importance of being true extends beyond personal development, catalysing intense transformations that resonate through our lives and shape the very world we inhabit.

Authenticity holds transformative potential, and its influence extends far beyond individual experiences. It can change lives, family dynamics and company values. By delving into the depths of our true selves, we unlock the power to form genuine connections with others. It enables us to transcend superficialities, to connect at a deep level and cultivate relationships built on trust, empathy and understanding. As we embrace our authentic selves, we inspire others to do the same, thereby creating a ripple effect that spreads further authenticity and acceptance throughout our communities.

Moreover, authenticity is a gateway to personal fulfilment and emotional wellbeing. When we honour our true desires, values and passions, we align our lives with our innermost aspirations. By embracing authenticity, we give ourselves permission to pursue what brings us joy and meaning, and this can lead to a deep sense of fulfilment and contentment. This journey of self-discovery and self-acceptance enhances our own wellbeing and radiates positive energy to uplift those around us.

In the context of our ever-evolving world, authenticity empowers us to have a positive effect in society. By embracing our authentic voices, we contribute to the creation of a compassionate and harmonious world that values and celebrates the inherent uniqueness of every individual. Being genuine in our actions emboldens us to challenge societal norms, to break free from limiting beliefs and advocate for what we believe in. It is through our authentic actions and expressions that we inspire change, foster inclusivity and create a world in which diverse perspectives and talents can thrive.

When we are authentic, we allow ourselves to be vulnerable and open with others, which can lead to deep and meaningful relationships. When we hide parts of ourselves or put up a façade, we can find ourselves struggling to connect with others at a deep level. When we learn to be comfortable with who we are, we give others permission to do the same, thereby promoting authentic and meaningful relationships.

When we live inauthentically, we may find ourselves living a life based on the expectations of others, rather than our own desires and passions. Conversely, when we embrace our true selves and live as we wish to be, not as we are told we ought to be, we are able to create a life that is truly our own and aligned with our values and passions.

CASE STUDY
Jenna finds fulfilment

For years, Jenna worked in a corporate job that she did not enjoy, simply because it had been drummed into her from an early age that this kind of role was expected of her. Jenna's parents were inclined to conform with societal expectations and they also did not have much in the way of financial resources. At school, Jenna loved art classes and aspired to be an artist, but her parents said that being an artist would not pay the bills and she really needed to stop dreaming about "that sort of stuff", otherwise she would always be disappointed. Jenna was convinced that pursuing a career in the arts was impractical and unlikely to lead to financial success.

As Jenna approached her thirtieth birthday, she realised that she was deeply unhappy with her corporate life and felt like she was wasting her potential. After some soul-searching, she decided to work part-time at her corporate job and pursue her passion for the arts. She started by taking painting classes and attending local art shows, and eventually began selling her own artworks. Over time Jenna found she was able to make a living from her artwork. Today she is a successful professional artist who has found deep fulfilment and purpose in her life. By embracing her true self, Jenna was able to tap into a sense of purpose and passion that had been missing from her life for years.

Authenticity promotes growth and development

When we are living genuinely, we are constantly growing and developing into better versions of ourselves. This is because we are able to identify areas for improvement and take action to pursue new experiences and opportunities that align with our true selves.

Living this way is a catalyst for growth and development as it encourages us to embrace our true selves and strive for personal and professional improvement. We are able to develop a deep understanding of our values, strengths and areas that may be improved. This self-awareness enables us to set meaningful goals and take deliberate actions that align with our true aspirations, thereby propelling us forward on a path of development.

Authenticity also fosters a mindset of curiosity and openness. When we embrace our real selves, we become receptive to new ideas, perspectives and experiences. We are willing to step outside of our comfort zones and explore unfamiliar territories, which often leads to personal and professional breakthroughs. By being open to growth and expansion, we unlock opportunities for learning, development and the acquisition of new skills.

Moreover, living in alignment with our values fuels intrinsic motivation, which is a powerful driver for growth and development. When we are true to ourselves, our actions are driven by genuine passion and enthusiasm. We are naturally inclined to invest time and effort into activities that resonate with our sincere desires and aspirations. This innate motivation fuels our commitment to continuous improvement and propels us to seek out challenges, embrace feedback and push our boundaries to achieve personal and professional growth.

Authenticity encourages us to seek personal and professional development that aligns with our values and interests. Rather than conforming to societal expectations or following a predetermined path, we have the freedom to explore and pursue our passions. By engaging in activities and endeavours that resonate with our authentic selves, we tap into a wellspring of motivation and enthusiasm that fuels our growth and development. Whether this means attending workshops, seeking mentors or pursuing further education, authenticity empowers us to make intentional choices that support our personal and professional growth.

It also promotes growth by encouraging self-reflection and self-evaluation. When we live in alignment with our values, we are attuned to our inner voice and emotions. This heightened self-understanding enables us to critically assess our strengths, weaknesses and areas for improvement, thereby supporting us to develop strategies to overcome obstacles and make progress. By regularly reflecting on our experiences and engaging in self-evaluation, we cultivate a growth mindset and embrace a proactive approach to personal and professional development.

In essence, authenticity is the soil in which personal growth and development flourish. By embracing our true selves, we unlock the potential for continuous learning, expansion and the pursuit of meaningful experiences that shape our journey of growth.

Authenticity improves working relationships

A survey conducted by the Australian Bureau of Statistics in April 2021 found that almost half (41 per cent) of Australian employees regularly worked from home, up from 32 per cent in 2019.[1] In the modern work landscape, authentic connections are crucial for effective collaboration and job satisfaction. However, the shift to remote work has made it harder to maintain these genuine relationships. As the boundaries between work and personal life blur, the need for meaningful connections and genuine engagement becomes increasingly apparent.

For us to be truly happy at work we must be able to bring our authentic selves to work, this includes when we are working from home. When we are genuine, we are able to connect with others at a deep level, not needing to hide behind a facade or trying to be someone we are not. The result can be relationships that are fulfilling at both the personal and professional levels. Being authentic at work has the power to significantly

---

1 Australian Bureau of Statistics (2022), Working time arrangements (webpage, last updated 14 December 2022). Accessed 26 September 2023, https://www.abs.gov.au/statistics/labour/earnings-and-working-conditions/working-arrangements/latest-release#working-time-arrangements

strengthen working relationships, thereby fostering a positive and collaborative environment. When people bring their true selves to the workplace, trust and genuineness can be cultivated among colleagues. By openly expressing their thoughts, ideas and concerns, workers can create an atmosphere that encourages honest communication and collaboration among colleagues. If everyone at work is authentic in their actions, it can promote a sense of psychological safety, enabling everyone to feel comfortable being themselves and sharing their unique perspectives without fear of judgement or retribution. While this is the ideal, we also need to understand that not everyone will feel safe to bring their true selves to work. There are a number of reasons for this, some of which I have covered later in this book such as lack of self-awareness, peer pressure and pressure to conform to name a few. What I have found is that if you are authentic, others who are also authentic will tend to gravitate towards you. People tend to recognise in someone an energy and spark that they wish to have or share.

Establishing genuine connections among colleagues can contribute to the formation of strong working relationships. Over time, this dynamic can enhance morale and interactions within the workplace. By revealing your genuine self in your professional environment, you can foster a deep personal connection with others that goes beyond surface-level exchanges. This deepening bond can encourage co-workers to offer assistance readily when you reach out for help.

Displaying a certain level of vulnerability, sharing personal experiences and showing empathy can contribute to cultivation of an atmosphere that engenders mutual understanding and support. I can say that in my current role I have personally experienced this transformation in the workplace. In contrasting, in past workplaces, I used to project a facade of contentment and reliability, positioning myself as the dependable, go-to person, just to avoid disappointing anyone. However, this facade eventually bred resentment and frustration, as I felt misunderstood by my colleagues. While we engaged in routine pleasantries such as discussing the weather or what we did on the weekends, no one truly took the initiative to genuinely connect.

Since I made the shift to being authentic in my work interactions, truly listening and enquiring about others, I am witnessing improvements in my interactions with those around me. I enjoy helping others who take an interest in what I am trying to achieve and I give more to those who show they care.

As I have transitioned towards being authentic in my work interactions – genuinely listening and showing interest in others – I have experienced fulfilling exchanges with my colleagues. I have discovered a newfound pleasure in assisting people who express genuine curiosity about the work I do, and I have become more generous with my efforts towards those who demonstrate care. This shift has also led me to value that my some of my co-workers feel they can relate to me and others on a deep level, and that this has cultivated a sense of mutual understanding and camaraderie. These genuine connections have played a pivotal role in enhancing teamwork, increased collaboration and, ultimately, a more positive work culture overall.

CASE STUDY
Improved working relationships with Jane and Peter

Jane and Peter were two people working with me on a major transportation project.

Jane was known for her genuine and open approach to work. For Jane, being her authentic self meant consistently communicating truthfully and respectfully with me and her colleagues. She openly shared her ideas and thoughts, provided constructive feedback and actively listened to others' perspectives. Jane was known to be helpful and insightful. I noticed that her colleagues appreciated her authenticity, as it fostered trust and transparency within the team. By encouraging open and honest dialogue, Jane had created an environment in which everyone felt comfortable expressing their thoughts and ideas. This free flowing of communication not only enhanced the group's problem-solving but also sparked creativity and innovation among the team members. It was a great team to work with.

Peter, on the other hand, always seemed distracted and distant. I wanted to understand why he seemed so distracted, so I invited him out for lunch one day. When I asked him about it, Peter admitted that he had been struggling to be present at work as he felt he did not belong at the company. Peter said he admired Jane, and noticed that everyone liked her, but colleagues were less interested in him and barely said good morning, let alone asked about his weekend. This had a negative effect on him, and his performance and work output were suffering as a result. I encouraged Peter to find a coach or a mentor to help him work through the issues he was experiencing. I suggested that this could help to improve his performance, or at the very least help him understand how to interact better with his colleagues. Peter reluctantly agreed to this advice and sought out a work performance coach. Over the following three months I saw a marked improvement in Peter's interactions within the team and he seemed happier at work. When I next caught up with him, he revealed that the coaching sessions were helping him to discover the benefits of embracing his authenticity in the workplace.

Peter tried some of the techniques suggested by his coach and began to embrace his own identity. He realised that his unique ideas and perspectives could make a valuable contribution to the team, and that he was not as harshly judged by his colleagues as he thought. By overcoming his fear of judgement, Peter began to actively participate in discussions, sharing his thoughts and insights, and offering creative solutions. His newfound authenticity inspired his colleagues, who appreciated his genuine contributions and recognised the value he brought to the team. The change from being reserved and hesitant to share his true thoughts at work, to being his authentic self was motivating. Peter's enthusiasm and passion was infectious, and encouraged his colleagues to bring their best selves to work.

Jane's and Peter's authentic approaches fostered a culture of collaboration and productivity in the workplace. Their genuine interactions created a positive work environment in which their team members felt heard, valued and respected. This encouraged people within the team to share their ideas and take ownership of their work, and led to improved levels of engagement and productivity.

As a result of Jane and Peter being authentic at work, their team developed improved problem-solving capabilities, enhanced creativity and effective decision-making. I noticed that their team members were also able to build strong bonds of trust, which enabled them to work seamlessly together, delegate tasks and leverage off each other's strengths.

This example demonstrates that being authentic at work can strengthen working relationships by fostering trust, genuine connections, credibility and innovation. In turn, this can create an environment in which everyone feels safe to express their true selves, and can lead to open communication, improved collaboration and a positive and productive work environment. By valuing and promoting authenticity, organisations can unlock the full potential of their employees and promote a culture that celebrates individuality and fosters strong and fulfilling working relationships.

There are countless stories of people who have embraced their authenticity and transformed their lives. Among these are the stories of Jenna, who left a corporate job to pursue her passion for the arts; Peter, who learned to express his true emotions and form deeper connections with others; and Lucy (see case study on page 36) who created a life aligned with her true passions and values. These stories offer powerful reminders of the importance of authenticity in our lives. As Oprah Winfrey once said "The biggest adventure you can ever take is to live the life of your dreams."[2] By embracing our true selves and living authentically, we can embark on that adventure and create a life that is truly our own.

---

2 What Oprah knows for sure about life's biggest adventure, *O: The Oprah Magazine*, July 2002. Accessed 1 September 2023, https://www.oprah.com/spirit/what-oprah-knows-for-sure-about-lifes-biggest-adventure#:~:text=The%20biggest%20adventure%20you%20can,and%20what%20you%20cannot%20do.

Barriers to authentic living

Exploring the intricate concept of authenticity unveils a complex interplay of factors that can hinder its full expression. Among these formidable barriers, the weight of societal norms and expectations often exerts a stifling force, impeding the uninhibited revelation of one's true self. The relentless pressure to conform to established norms and predefined roles can obscure our genuine desires and passions, compelling us to trade our unique identities for predetermined and often confining images.

Another significant hurdle that looms in the pursuit of authenticity is the pervasive "fear of missing out" (or FoMO). In an age characterised by being constantly "on" and the relentless comparisons fostered on social media platforms, the line between genuine aspirations and societal trends can become blurred. Ceaseless comparison of ourselves with others, especially through curated online platforms, can sow the seeds of insecurity and anxiety, gradually eroding our ability to make choices that align with our authentic selves. This fear-driven pursuit of external validation can drive us away from our intrinsic path, ensnaring us in a cycle of unfulfilling pursuits and reinforcing the barriers to authenticity.

The echoing whispers of self-doubt cast yet another shadow on the path to embracing authenticity. The nagging uncertainty about our self-worth and capabilities can paralyse our expressions, decisions and pursuits. This self-doubt undermines the self-assuredness required to break free from the shackles of societal expectations and to encourage us to venture into the uncharted territory of authentic living. A lack of self-confidence not only erodes our ability to make choices rooted in our true convictions, but also diminishes our capacity to navigate the often turbulent waters of life with unwavering resolve.

Moreover, the absence of knowing our own values and beliefs sets a fundamental barrier in the quest for authenticity. Without a deep understanding of what drives and motivates us, it can be difficult to differentiate authentic choices from external influences. This lack of self-knowledge can lead us down paths that do not resonate with our true selves, thereby perpetuating a cycle of dissatisfaction and thwarting our progress towards authentic living. The societal framework further compounds this issue, as it often dictates external expectations and norms that obscure our inner compass, leaving us in a constant struggle between societal conformity and genuine self-expression.

Yet, in this intricate dance between conformity and authenticity, there is hope. Our journey through the pages of this book serves as a guide to dismantling these formidable barriers. Together, we embark on a voyage of introspection and self-compassion, and embrace vulnerability as the catalysts for transformation. As we navigate the terrain of self-discovery, we cultivate the tools and insights necessary to break free from conformity's grip, banish self-doubt and defy the constraints of societal expectations.

Fear not, Dear Reader, for as we delve deeper into these pages, the path to authenticity becomes illuminated. By embracing your true self, you will stand resilient against the pressures of conformity, and develop a deep sense of self-confidence and trust in your intuitive wisdom. Armed with newfound clarity and an unwavering commitment to authenticity, you will emerge empowered to lead a life that is an unapologetic reflection of your unique essence.

2

The Authenticity Model: Values, Trust and Self-Awareness

As I contemplated the essence of being authentic in my own life, I was prompted to explore my core values. By doing this I was able to construct a meaningful model that encapsulated its significance to me.

My own definition of authenticity is the degree to which a person's conduct harmonises with their principles and ambitions, even when confronted with external pressures that urge them to conform with societal norms.

At the centre of personal development and the desire for meaningful connections lies a fundamental notion links values, trust and self-awareness, depicted in Figure 1. Authenticity epitomises the purest manifestation of one's true self; it encompasses a sincere alignment of a person's values, actions and engagements. Authenticity is the cornerstone of trust: those who exhibit authenticity are perceived as dependable, credible and genuine. It is interwoven with self-awareness and demands of the individual a reflective comprehension of their own values and convictions. This convergence of authenticity, values, trust and self-awareness generates a dynamic interplay of factors that shape our relationships, decisions and overall sense of identity.

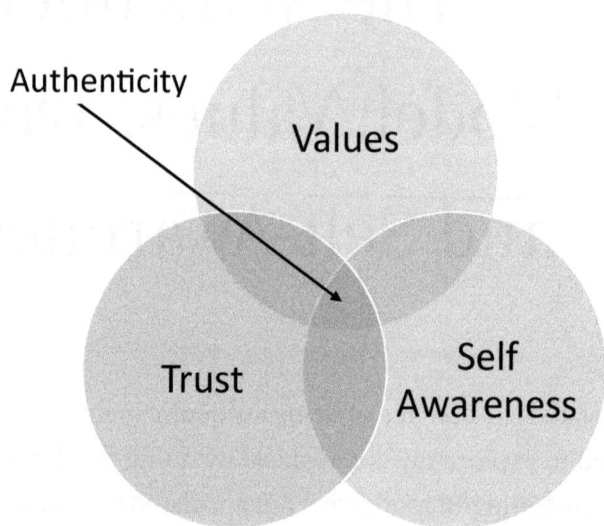

Figure 1: The Authenticity Model

When authenticity is present, trust is cultivated naturally. People who are authentic inspire confidence through their consistent and transparent behaviour, leading others to feel secure about relying on them. In the context of relationships, the authenticity–trust alliance forms the bedrock of meaningful connections, enabling individuals to share their vulnerabilities, express emotions and engage in open dialogue. This heightened level of trust fosters deeper connections and encourages reciprocity, since the act of being authentic often invites others to reciprocate by revealing their true selves.

Furthermore, the interplay of authenticity, self-awareness and values creates a virtuous cycle of self-discovery and growth. Authenticity requires a reflective knowledge of one's values, and this introspective journey fosters self-appreciation. As people delve into their core values and beliefs, they develop an understanding of who they are and what truly matters to them. This enhanced self-cognisance, in turn, fuels authenticity, thereby empowering the person to express themselves genuinely and to cultivate connections with others who share similar values. Thus, the cycle continues, as deeper connections amplify self-knowledge and reinforce the importance of staying true to one's values.

Cultivating personal values

Our personal values are the fundamental beliefs that shape our decisions and actions, influenced by our upbringing, culture and life experiences. Considered together, our values offer a clear framework that can assist in navigating life's complexities; for example, by helping us prioritise what is truly significant. These values steer our choices, relationships and life goals; they nurture authenticity and a sense of purpose. Living in harmony with our values enables us to pursue what genuinely resonates, rather than conform to external pressures. This alignment fosters a heightened sense of purpose and fulfillment, enabling us to pursue our passions and lead lives that truly reflect our true selves. Chapter 4 discusses how you can identify your own values.

CASE STUDY
Aligning with my own values

Over the course of 23 years, a substantial chapter of my career was dedicated to a role that did not correspond completely with my inner calling. I was driven by the pursuit of financial stability and the allure of external recognition. Remarkably, I excelled within this capacity, progressively advancing from recruit to the position of Naval Lieutenant. Despite achieving recognition and financial stability, an enduring sense of emptiness lingered. Beneath the surface, an earnest yearning for a different path pulled at the threads of my aspirations – a desire to nurture individuals to reach their highest potential through coaching and mentoring. Well-meaning friends advised me against veering from the established route I had carved, because of the uncertainties this presented.

In spite of these uncertainties, I made the pivotal decision to depart from the military and follow my passion. Even then, I found myself not fully aligned with my core values. Although I was inching closer to living according to my values, the feeling remained that unadulterated happiness was elusive. A few years ago, I left my engineering career and summoned the courage to embark on a quest of self-discovery. This moment heralded the start of my transformation into a coach and mentor. While I had been coaching and mentoring for nearly a decade, I had regarded this work as personal pursuits rather than aspects of a conceivable professional path.

Fortified by newfound courage, I was able to relinquish my engineering role and wholeheartedly embrace a new direction in my professional life. This involved writing and deep learning, necessitating a substantial shift from my comfort zone. I enrolled in comprehensive coaching courses to deepen my understanding of the field. In parallel, I began writing blogs, developing an online presence and publishing content across digital platforms. I found that my genuine approach resonated powerfully with others, inciting them to explore their own passions. My writing evolved into a wellspring of inspiration that roused dormant creativity within those I engaged with.

These changes were transformative and sparked a rejuvenated sense of purpose within me. My sense of happiness and fulfilment flourished. Each day I awoke propelled by the sheer delight of being able to articulate and exchange my musings while assisting others on their life journeys. From this strong alignment between my aspirations and actions emerged a deep feeling of contentment. My transformation did not go unnoticed. People in my inner circle commented on my newfound sense of wellbeing and the radiance that seemed to emanate from my interactions. This transformation was no coincidence; it was a testament to the power of embracing my true self, unearthing my creativity and aligning my actions with my core values.

As my journey continues, I find myself not just embracing authenticity for my own sake, but also becoming a beacon for others – a source of motivation and inspiration. Through coaching, mentoring and education, I have woven authenticity into the fabric of my professional life. The cycle of growth, connection and positive change continues to flourish, setting the stage for a more purposeful and fulfilling existence. While I have since revisited the field of engineering, it has been from a people-centric approach: as an educator, coach and mentor for succeeding generations of engineers and women in STEM.

Authenticity breeds trust

Trust is formed through consistent actions, open communication and shared experiences. Trust helps to foster reliance on others' integrity and abilities, which is essential for collaboration and the development of emotional bonds. Trust is a cornerstone value for many organisations.

A study undertaken by Deloitte researchers has found trust plays a pivotal role in driving engagement and employee morale. Employees who trust their employers are not only 260 per cent more motivated to work but also exhibit 41 per cent lower rates of absenteeism and are 50 per cent less likely to seek alternative employment.[3] However, the disheartening truth is that approximately 25 per cent of workers lack trust in their employers. Compounding this issue, most employers overestimate the level of trust within their workforce by nearly 40 per cent. This misalignment in trust is a significant contributing factor to the decline in worker engagement.

Employer authenticity matters because it cultivates an environment in which employees feel safe to voice their opinions, concerns and ideas, and develop a sense of trust with their employers. When employees perceive their employers as authentic and transparent, they are more likely to speak up, share their perspectives and actively contribute to the organisation's growth and innovation. This open and collaborative culture fosters a sense of psychological safety and enables the organisation to tap into the diverse knowledge and insights of its employees, thereby driving creativity and problem-solving.

---

3   Ashley Reichheld & Amelia Dunlop (2023), How to build a high trust workplace, MIT Sloan Management Review (website), 23 January. Accessed 1 September 2023, https://sloanreview.mit.edu/article/how-to-build-a-high-trust-workplace/#:~:text=Our%20research%20shows%20that%20trust,don't%20trust%20their%20employer

Authenticity breeds trust and credibility in the workplace. When people consistently show up as their authentic selves, they are perceived as genuine and reliable. Colleagues and superiors value their authenticity and view it as a sign of integrity. Authenticity also builds credibility by aligning actions with values and fostering transparency. Trust and credibility are essential for building strong working relationships, as colleagues rely on one another to fulfil their responsibilities and achieve shared goals.

Therefore, when we bring our true selves to work each day, others are more likely to trust us, as they know that we are being genuine and honest. This can be especially important in professional settings, where trust is critical for building strong working relationships between clients and co-workers, and helps achieve success. Authenticity builds trust in several ways. It creates a sense of consistency and reliability. When we consistently show up as our authentic selves, our actions align with our words, and others can rely on us to be open and sincere. This consistency builds trust over time, as people know they can predict and rely on our behaviour. They trust that we will be true to ourselves and transparent in our interactions.

Erosion of trust

On the flip side, a negative consequence of not being authentic is the erosion of trust within the team or organisation. When people are not genuine in their communication, it creates an atmosphere of uncertainty and doubt. Without authenticity, team members may question the motives behind the information shared, may suspect hidden agendas or feel unsure about the accuracy of the messages conveyed.

In such an environment, open and honest dialogue becomes compromised. Without the foundation of authenticity and trust, team members may hesitate to express their thoughts, ideas and concerns openly. They may fear the potential repercussions or doubt the sincerity of their colleagues' responses. This lack of transparency stifles collaboration, inhibits effective problem-solving and hinders the development of meaningful relationships within the team.

The absence of sincerity can lead to misunderstandings and misinterpretations. When people are not honest in their communication, it can be challenging to discern their true intentions or motivations. This ambiguity can give rise to conflicts, misaligned expectations and strained relationships among team members. Without the clarity and trust that authenticity brings, misunderstandings can escalate, resulting in decreased productivity, increased tensions and even damaged working relationships.

Additionally, the lack of honesty can contribute to a culture of secrecy and guardedness. When individuals do not feel comfortable being their legitimate selves, they may resort to concealing information or withholding their true opinions. This undermines collaboration, hampers innovation and stifles the free flow of ideas. It also creates a culture in which people feel the need to constantly second-guess and question the genuineness of their colleagues' communication, and can lead to a breakdown in trust and cohesion.

Being honest at work demonstrates respect for others' uniqueness and encourages a culture of acceptance. When we embrace our authenticity, we inherently value and respect the legitimacy of others. By accepting and appreciating people for who they truly are, we create a safe and inclusive environment where trust can flourish. Authenticity encourages open-mindedness and celebrates diversity, which in turn builds trust among colleagues who feel seen, heard and valued for their unique contributions.

Developing self-awareness

Self-awareness is our ability to recognise and comprehend our own thoughts, emotions and actions. It can lead to a deep understanding of ourselves and how we interact with the world. Self-awareness involves undertaking reflective practices to uncover our strengths, weaknesses and motivations, thereby fostering personal growth and informed decision-making.

Living authentically requires you to be self-aware and in tune with your thoughts, feelings and intentions. Your self-awareness is a powerful tool that positively influences your work output. By being in tune with your thoughts, feelings and intentions, you can make intentional choices and decisions in your professional life. You become aware of your true motivations and aspirations, and can pursue work that aligns with your values and brings you fulfilment. This alignment between your authentic self and your work cultivates a sense of purpose and drive, fuelling your productivity and commitment to achieving meaningful outcomes.

Moreover, having knowledge of yourself enables you to identify and manage your limitations and areas for growth. By acknowledging your weaknesses and seeking opportunities for improvement, you can proactively develop new skills and seek support or mentorship. Self-knowledge encourages a growth mindset, which strengthens our ability to embrace challenges, take calculated risks and continuously strive for excellence. It also enhances the ability to collaborate effectively with others, as we open ourselves to feedback, diverse perspectives and a willingness to learn and adapt.

By understanding yourself at a deeper level, you can make intentional choices that align your work with your values, and thereby are empowered to pursue a fulfilling career. Positive self-perception is liberating; it enables you to identify, understand and address your imperfections, and this in turn fosters further growth that motivates you towards continuous improvement and achievement of your professional goals. Ultimately, the combination of authenticity and self-awareness creates a powerful foundation for your personal and professional success.

CASE STUDY
Lucy becomes self-aware

Lucy was passionate about supporting renewable energy initiatives. Her curiosity for sustainable solutions ran deep and drove her desire to contribute meaningfully.

When we met, Lucy was employed at an engineering firm that had no ties with the renewable energy sector. Thus, despite her enjoyment of engineering, Lucy was not pursuing the goals she aspired to. This misalignment between her personal values and her work left her feeling unfulfilled and uninspired.

Lucy engaged me as her coach, seeking assistance to clarify her career direction. Through introspection, she unearthed her authentic calling. She identified her passion for creating a greener future and yearned to align her career with this purpose.

With this newfound clarity, Lucy took the bold step of seeking opportunities in the renewable energy sector. With my support, she secured a role at a clean-energy startup that specialised in innovative solar technologies. In her new position, Lucy gained a revitalised sense of purpose and alignment with her true self. Today, her passion and expertise shine through as she contributes ideas and solutions that drive sustainable energy practices.

Lucy's authenticity and self-awareness have deeply influenced her work. She has immersed herself in her projects, going the extra mile to ensure the successful implementation of renewable energy solutions. Her dedication has become a catalyst for others in her workplace. She has inspired colleagues through her positive approach and this has led to a collaborative work atmosphere – a change that is palpable even in our coaching conversations. Lucy's commitment to growth has led her to proactively seek professional development to gain new knowledge and skills. She now attends conferences, engages wholeheartedly in workshops and is cultivating a network of like-minded professionals. Her self-understanding has empowered Lucy to leverage her strengths while continuously seeking to expand her knowledge and expertise.

In this scenario, Lucy's authenticity and self-awareness led her to pursue a career in the renewable energy sector, thereby aligning her work with her values. She has gained job satisfaction and a deep sense of fulfillment. Lucy's authentic approach now drives her to excel and to contribute innovative solutions in the field of sustainable engineering.

Challenges arising from lack of authentic living

Throughout my coaching career, I have encountered many people living inauthentic lives. Ironically, I too fell into that category for a significant period in my life, and the consequences were severe, affecting both my physical and mental wellbeing. For years, I dedicated myself to pleasing others and conforming to societal expectations.

In June 2010, during my third year of engineering studies, a pivotal moment occurred. At that time, I was a single parent, shouldering the responsibility of raising my two daughters, then aged 7 and 9 years. The challenges of juggling parenthood and academic pursuits were taking their toll, physically and mentally. I was overwhelmed by stress. My father had suffered a stroke and was now living with me, which placed an additional burden on my already stretched resources.

Since the military was funding my education, passing all my subjects every semester was a strict requirement. I made the misguided decision to withdraw from a particularly difficult subject, fearing the prospect of failure. The implications of this decision were questioned at a meeting with the academic review board. The harsh criticism of a panel member whom I deeply respected pushed me to the brink of dropping out entirely from university study. Imposter syndrome, that nagging feeling of being inadequate, was my constant companion as the weight of striving to meet the expectations of others led me astray from my authentic self.

Seeking guidance and clarity, I wandered into a second-hand bookshop, allowing fate to guide me to the self-help section. It was there that I stumbled upon a worn-out book by Dr Wayne W. Dyer. The title, *Your Erroneous Zones* (published by Avon Books in 1977), resonated deeply. I felt an immediate connection to the words on the pages. Little did I know that this tattered book would become a catalyst for my journey towards authenticity and self-discovery.

In this book, Dr Dyer explored the concept of personal growth and the importance of taking control of one's own life. He focused on identifying and overcoming self-destructive thought patterns and behaviours that hinder personal development and happiness, and offered practical strategies and insights to help people break free from limiting beliefs, societal conditioning and external expectations.

Dr Dyer also emphasised the significance of being true to oneself and living in alignment with one's values and desires. He encouraged readers to let go of the need for approval from others and to trust their own instincts and inner wisdom. He emphasised that true happiness and fulfilment come from embracing one's authenticity and that one's choices should be based on personal integrity rather than seeking external validation.

Inspired by this newfound awareness, I attended a seminar presented by Dr Dyer when he visited Australia, coincidentally the following month, and delved into the concept of authenticity. As I immersed myself in his words, and embraced my own inner wisdom, a deep resonance stirred within me. It was as though a light had been "switched on", illuminating the realisation that I had been living a life dictated by the expectations of others. That I had been living detached from my true essence.

Determined to reclaim my freedom, I embarked on the journey of self-discovery. I started by addressing the challenges I was facing in my studies. I acknowledged that until then my choices had been driven by external pressures and the expectations of others. With a renewed sense of self, I began to assert my opinions and ideas with greater confidence. I no longer felt bound by the fear of judgement or the pressure to conform. In an outward reflection of this change, I consciously adjusted my wardrobe choices, opting for clothes that truly reflected my personal style and made me feel comfortable and empowered.

These small yet significant changes marked the beginning of my transformation. By embracing my true self, I discovered the freedom to live life on my own terms, guided by my own values and aspirations. This newfound alignment with my own genuineness not only enhanced my sense of fulfilment but also set the stage for further personal growth and development. It paved the way towards a more authentic and purposeful existence. But it would be 10 years before I fully shed the chains of conformity and embraced authentic living.

Benefits of living an authentic life

The first noticeable benefit of embracing an authentic life is improved self-confidence. Authenticity invites you to be comfortable in your own skin, free from the need to hide your true self or pretend to be someone you are not. This inner alignment leads to a sense of deep confidence and inner peace, a pride in knowing and being who you truly are.

Living authentically enriches your relationships and friendships. When you stay true to yourself, you naturally attract people who share your values and beliefs. When you are no longer trying to please everyone, you begin to forge meaningful connections with those who truly matter.

In living authentically, you will notice improved mental and physical health. By shedding the constant pressure to meet others' expectations, stress and anxiety are reduced. This liberation enables you to fully engage in the present, which can lead to better sleep, reduced physical tension and an overall sense of improved wellbeing.

Embracing authenticity nurtures self-love and self-acceptance. By releasing the need to present a façade, you genuinely begin to appreciate your true self. This self-acceptance fosters inner peace and a positive self-image that values your unique qualities and strengths.

Authenticity streamlines your decision-making. As you gain liberation from having to conform to external pressures, you gain clarity in recognising your desires and values. This clarity empowers you to make choices that are in alignment with your true self. You are driven towards a fulfilling life of integrity.

Authentic living bolsters your resilience. By understanding your identity and values, your strength and adaptability deepen and anchor your convictions when you face challenges.

Finally, living authentically liberates you from the burden of meeting others' expectations. This freedom lets you prioritise what truly matters. It enables you to express yourself genuinely, and to pursue your passions so that you can lead a purpose-driven existence.

Ultimately, authenticity inspires trust and respect from others. Your genuine self radiates integrity and draws people who value authenticity. This foundation establishes meaningful connections and nurturing trust and respect in relationships.

In the words of the American poet and philosopher Ralph Waldo Emerson, "To be yourself in a world that is constantly trying to make you something else is the greatest accomplishment".[4]

I encourage you to take a step back and reflect on whether you are living authentically. Are you being true to yourself, or are you conforming to the expectations of others? Remember, living authentically is not always easy, but the benefits are worthwhile. Choose to live in a way that is true to yourself and watch as your life is transformed.

---

4 Ralph Waldo Emerson (2014) *Ralph Waldo Emerson – Essays: To be yourself in a world that is constantly trying to make you something else is the greatest accomplishment,* A Word To The Wise Publishers (online only through Amazon)

3

Navigating the Tensions
of Conformity

Authenticity resonates deeply within many of us. It calls us to be genuine, to stay true to ourselves amidst the pressures and expectations of society. Authenticity is about breaking free from the shackles of conformity and embracing our unique essence. As the acclaimed researcher and storyteller Brené Brown once expressed it: "Authenticity is the daily practice of letting go of who we think we're supposed to be and embracing who we are."[1]

As we explore the depths of authenticity, it becomes evident that conformity stands as its opposing force, compelling us to shape ourselves to fit societal expectations. The comparison of authenticity and conformity is not only that they represent a dichotomy, but also that we are invited to consider the complex

---

1 Brené Brown (2010), *The Gifts of Imperfection,* Hazelden Publishing.

interplay between our innate desire to be true to ourselves and the external pressures that push us towards assimilation.

Happiness and the allure of conformity

Imagine a conversation between two friends, Suzanna and Hayley, as they discuss the challenges of being authentic and the allure of conforming to society's expectations.

> **Suzanna:** You know, Hayley, embracing authenticity has been quite a challenge for me. I sometimes struggle with what I want to do and what is expected of me. I feel like breaking free from the expectations society has placed on me, and I want to find the courage to express my true self.
>
> **Hayley:** I'm hearing you, Suzanna. But let's not forget the allure of conformity. Society bombards us with images of what success, happiness and fulfilment should look like, so I can understand how tempting it is to conform and shape ourselves to fit those ideals, even if it means sacrificing our authenticity.
>
> **Suzanna:** That is true. I am often afraid of being judged or rejected if I deviate from the norm. The pressure to conform can be overwhelming. Sometimes I feel like I am wearing a mask that suppresses my genuine thoughts and emotions.
>
> **Hayley:** Me too! I find myself caught in a tug-of-war between my innate need for acceptance and my longing to stay true to who I really am. I know it takes strength

and self-awareness to resist the gravitational pull of conformity and embrace my unique essence, but I think I can do it – most days.

Suzanna: I couldn't agree more, Hayley. The task of decoding our authentic identity requires us to reflect deeply. I think we need to unravel the layers of social conditioning and societal expectations that have shaped us, to discover our true values, passions and beliefs.

Hayley: Absolutely. I think it is time we take action and reclaim our power to define our own narratives and live in alignment with our core truths. Only then can we experience genuine fulfilment and create meaningful connections with others.

This chapter seeks to untangle the complexities that often obscure our true selves. By shedding light on the interplay between authenticity and conformity, it offers valuable insights into the forces that shape our identities and strategies to navigate the delicate balance between staying true to ourselves and fitting into the world around us.

I enjoy reading self-help books and learning more about how our brains work. This stems from not having had strong role models throughout my life, and I have had to seek help from books to discover what I could be doing better. One such book was *The Happiness Trap*, by Dr Russ Harris.[2] In this book, Dr Harris explored how to find genuine happiness by embracing authenticity and aligning our actions with our core values. The essence of the book was the false notion of being able to pursue and achieve

---

2 Russ Harris (2007), *The Happiness Trap*, Exisle Publishing.

true happiness, bearing in mind its relationship with authenticity and conformity. Dr Harris challenged conventional notions of happiness and offered a fresh perspective on finding genuine fulfilment in a society that often promotes external validation and the need to conform. He also argued that the relentless pursuit of pleasure and avoidance of discomfort can cause us to become trapped in a cycle of dissatisfaction, and can perpetuate a false sense of happiness. By constantly seeking external validation and conforming to societal expectations, we can lose touch with our true selves and what brings us genuine joy.

Questioning societal norms

Embracing authenticity requires us to question societal norms and ideologies. This entails the cultivation of an open mind. We must actively seek diverse perspectives and critically evaluate our own convictions. Our true beliefs are rooted in personal exploration, and are uncovered through reflection and the courage to form opinions that align with our authentic selves. By embracing our beliefs, we align our actions and choices with our core values, thereby fostering a sense of congruence and purpose in our lives.

Disregarding our true selves and succumbing to external pressures can have detrimental consequences. This is particularly evident in how we present ourselves in the world: what we wear and how we behave in certain situations. It is common to find ourselves conforming to societal expectations or fashion trends that do not align with our natural style. I discovered this about myself during my time in the military. The strict regulations governing employment in the military requires people to conform to the notions of being upstanding citizens and upholding values higher than those expected of the general public. This dictated the appropriate behaviour, hairstyle, make-up choices and even the jewellery we were allowed to wear. It also went beyond physical appearance, to expectations about how we should behave to gain acceptance from our peers and to project a certain image to the outside world as a member of the military. It is important to understand why this is required in an organisation such as the military. However, over a period of time, the strict rules of conformity can have negative effects on people who do not have a strong sense of self.

As I followed the prescribed standards during my military career, I unknowingly allowed them to seep into my personal life, mainly because I knew nothing different. Following my time in the military I experienced a deep sense of not fitting into society; once I transitioned to civilian life there seemed to be conflicting expectations of me. The struggle to reconcile my authentic self with the societal norms I had internalised in the military created a dissonance that affected my confidence and sense of belonging. This, in turn, influenced my parenting style, social behaviour and other areas of my life. It was not until I began to prioritise my personal growth and sought to realign my values that I was able to break free from the conformity of military life.

It is crucial to realise the potential effects of neglecting our authentic selves in favour of conforming to external expectations. By suppressing our true identities, we risk losing touch with our unique essence and limiting our personal growth. It is through embracing our authenticity, even in the face of societal pressures, that we can rediscover a sense of belonging and forge a path that aligns with our genuine desires and values.

There may be times when conformity is necessary or beneficial. As already mentioned, being a member of the military is one example; others include being a police officer, paramedic or doctor etc. For safety and security reasons, it may be important to adhere to certain norms or expectations. When military personnel follow established procedures and guidelines, it can help to minimise the risk of errors and accidents. By adhering to a set of established practices, they can work together efficiently and effectively, which can ultimately save lives.

However, it is important to note that conformity should not be taken to the extreme. Blindly following orders without question can lead to a lack of critical thinking and personal initiative. It is important for everyone to maintain their own sense of identity and agency; to maintain a sense of integrity and to make choices that align with our own values and beliefs as far as possible.

In the military, conforming was a constant expectation. It was a strict environment that prioritised following rules over independence. During my service, I faced challenges in understanding my own identity and aspirations because years of conforming had disconnected me from my authentic self. This struggle, however, did not solely stem from my military experience. It had deeper roots in my unconventional upbringing by a single parent, my father, which deviated from societal norms in the 1970s and 1980s.

In my childhood, my father's strict parenting style and the prevailing societal expectations of that era shaped my worldview.

As children, we were taught to be silent observers, to suppress our emotions and withhold our thoughts and opinions. Conformity became deeply ingrained within me from an early age, leaving little room for self-expression or the exploration of my own beliefs and aspirations. Consequently, I found myself grappling with a sense of having lost my identity and a lack of clarity regarding my own desires and goals.

Acknowledging the influence of family, and societal expectations and conformity, is pivotal in reclaiming our authentic selves. By understanding the ways in which external influences have shaped our lives, we can begin to break free from the limitations they impose. Embracing our true identities, desires and uniqueness enables us to tap into our untapped potential for growth, creativity and fulfilment. It is a journey of self-discovery and self-acceptance, whereby we unlearn the patterns of conformity and rekindle the flames of our unique essence.

CASE STUDY
Tiana rejects societal norms

Tiana had always been fascinated by the inner workings of machines and computers. As a child she loved tinkering with her own devices, taking them apart to see how they worked, and putting them back together again. She was encouraged by her parents to pursue what she enjoyed, so it was no surprise to anyone when Tiana decided to pursue a degree in engineering.

But as she started her journey through university, Tiana began to feel the pressure of societal norms and expectations. She was one of only a handful of women in her study program, and the constant comments from her male classmates and lecturers began to take their toll on her confidence. Soon, Tiana felt like she did not belong in this male-dominated field and that she needed to fit in by conforming to their expectations.

She started dressing differently, wearing less make-up and more "masculine" clothes, in an effort to be accepted by her male peers. She stopped speaking up in class and stopped sharing her unique ideas and perspectives, fearing they would not be taken seriously. She even started questioning her own abilities as an engineer, thinking that maybe she was not cut out for this profession after all.

It was not until her final year, during an internship at a tech company, that Tiana recognised how much she had been holding herself back. Her supervisor, a successful engineer, noticed how quiet and reserved Tiana was and encouraged her to speak up and share her ideas. She reminded Tiana that her unique perspective and ideas were valuable and that she should not be afraid to speak her mind.

Tiana took this advice to heart and began to shed her conformist tendencies. She dressed in a way that felt comfortable to her, rather than what she thought others expected. She spoke up in class and shared her ideas, and found that her classmates and lecturers respected her for it. She even started a women's engineering club on campus, creating a safe space for other women to pursue their passions in a male-dominated field.

As Tiana approached graduation, she appreciated how much she had grown and developed by embracing her true self. She realised that she had missed out on some opportunities to learn by conforming to societal norms and expectations, but now she was proud of who she was and confident in her abilities as an engineer. She knew that the road ahead would still be challenging, but she was ready to face it as her authentic self.

My own experience and that of Tiana serve as powerful reminders of the perils of conforming to societal norms and expectations, a phenomenon that is more prevalent than we may realise. The truth is, we all find ourselves wearing masks in certain social settings, driven by the fear of judgement and the desire to fit in. By succumbing to this conformity, Tiana and I inadvertently stifled our own potential. Fortunately, we each reached a point of awareness that enabled us to gain fresh insights into ourselves and able to uncover new opportunities for growth.

Conforming to societal norms and expectations not only hampers our personal development but also hinders our ability to express our true selves. It transforms us into mere followers, devoid of individuality and oblivious to our own unique capabilities and possibilities.

The effects of conformity

The influence of conformity on our lives, both on the personal and the collective levels, should not be underestimated. As we conform to societal norms and expectations, we can find ourselves facing the pressure to suppress our unique identities and assimilate.

Another author whose work I respect is Australian social researcher, author and commentator Hugh Mackay. He is widely recognised for his research in the field of social psychology and his insightful observations on human behaviour and societal trends. In his book, *The Art of Belonging*,[3] Professor Mackay explored belonging in the context of societal pressure to conform. He

---

3 Hugh Mackay (2014), *The Art of Belonging*, Pan Macmillan.

examined how conformity can influence our sense of belonging, and its effects on our individual and collective wellbeing.

These ideas resonated deeply within me, particularly the complexities of conforming to social expectations and the inherent tension between conformity and authentic self-expression. I appreciate Prof Mackay's challenge of the notion that belonging requires complete conformity; he emphasised the importance of finding a balance between fitting in and staying true to oneself.

Throughout his book, Prof Mackay offered insights into the negative consequences of excessive conformity, such as the suppression of individuality and the erosion of personal values and beliefs. He encouraged readers to critically evaluate the societal pressures that dictate conformity, and highlighted the importance of embracing one's authentic self. He offered practical guidance for navigating the tension between conformity and belonging, including strategies for cultivating a sense of belonging while maintaining personal authenticity, such as finding like-minded people or communities that support personal expression and value diversity.

I read *The Art of Belonging* as a call to action, urging readers to resist the pressure to blindly conform and instead to foster environments that encourage individuality, empathy and inclusivity. In it, Prof Mackay reminded us that true belonging is not about sacrificing our uniqueness but rather about creating spaces in which everyone feels accepted, respected and valued for their authentic selves.

Cognitive bias and masks as barriers to authenticity

As we seek to conform, we may find ourselves wearing different "masks" that help us fit in with our social circles, such as work, school, family and sports teams. These masks act as barriers that separate our true selves from the outside world. While they provide a sense of belonging, they also create disconnection and inner conflict. They may cause us to suppress our authentic voices and compromise our values, hindering genuine connections.

In work environments, it is common to don a mask that conforms to professional and workplace expectations and norms. We adopt a professional persona (e.g. respected engineer), suppressing aspects of our personality that do not align with the established corporate culture. I have witnessed with in all the various industries in which I have worked. Of note is the presence of a phenomenon called "social desirability bias", whereby people strive to present themselves in a favourable light that conforms with social norms. Others modify or conceal their true thoughts, feelings or behaviours to fit what is deemed socially or professionally acceptable. These behaviours can hinder us from expressing our genuine opinions or staying true to ourselves, as we fear judgement or rejection.

Another cognitive phenomenon that encourages conformity and hinders authenticity is known as "confirmation bias". This is the tendency to seek or interpret information in a way that confirms our existing beliefs or preconceived notions about something. For example, if someone believes all politicians are untrustworthy and only pays attention to news stories that confirm this belief, they are exhibiting confirmation bias. This is because people who hold a strong bias or belief about something selectively pay attention to information that supports that bias or belief while dismissing or ignoring contradictory evidence. This can hinder authenticity by preventing us from considering alternative perspectives or being open to changing our views. In a professional environment, confirmation bias can undermine authenticity. It leads people to seek information that aligns with their existing beliefs, limiting their openness to different perspectives. This hampers personal growth and restricts sincere expression. It also hinders genuine interactions and collaborations by dismissing alternative opinions and undervaluing diverse contributions.

Cognitive bias and diversity

In-group bias, a tendency to favour those within our social group, reinforces conformity and limits exposure to diverse perspectives. This type of bias can lead to exclusion and prevent us from authentically engaging with others who differ from us.

Within our familial relationships, we often feel compelled to wear yet another mask to adhere to family traditions and expectations. This can result in suppressing our true desires and opinions, sacrificing our authenticity for the sake of maintaining harmony within the family unit.

The accumulation of these masks and biases generates a sense of fragmentation within ourselves. We begin to question our true identity beneath the layers of conformity. This internal disconnection not only affects our self-perception but also hampers our ability to form deep and meaningful connections with others. We yearn for authentic interactions based on mutual understanding and acceptance, but the masks we wear prevent us from experiencing genuine connections.

To break free from this cycle, it is essential to recognise the influence of conformity and bias on our authenticity. By challenging societal norms, embracing diverse perspectives and valuing our uniqueness, we can begin to shed the masks and reconnect with our true selves. Recognising the many different masks, we wear and the influence they have on us is vitally important in reclaiming our authenticity. It requires self-reflection, introspection and the courage to step out of our comfort zones. In doing so, we foster genuine connections with others, based on mutual understanding, acceptance and the celebration of our authentic selves. This in turn, enables us to live fulfilling and meaningful lives, both for ourselves and in our relationships with others.

The importance of self-awareness in resisting conformity

Self-awareness is a vital component in resisting conformity and embracing authenticity. As a woman working in a male-dominated industry, I have experienced the pressure to conform to societal norms and expectations. However, as I have matured, I have learned to appreciate the daily pressures placed upon me, and I try to make conscious choices that align with my values and my authentic self.

Developing an appreciation of what motivates me has enabled me to identify my strengths and weaknesses so that I can use them in positive ways. For example, on the one hand, I have recognised that I am empathetic and intuitive, and this has helped me build strong relationships with colleagues and clients. On the other hand, I also know that I struggle with perfectionism, which has sometimes led me to set unrealistic expectations for myself.

By practising mindfulness, I have learned to manage my perfectionistic tendencies. To learn more about this concept, turn to Chapter 8. For the most part when practising mindfulness, I aim to focus on progress, rather than perfection. I learned this by reading James Clear's famous book, *Atomic Habits*,[4] which advocates to embracing a '2-minute' rule. This rule involves breaking tasks into small, manageable steps. It helps to prevent overwhelm and fosters consistent progress. Focusing on process over outcome aligns with the idea of accepting imperfection and promoting a growth mindset. Iterative improvement, a cornerstone of Clear's book, encouraged readers to embrace mistakes as learning opportunities, thereby effectively reducing the grip of perfectionism. Techniques such as tracking habits and making gradual adjustments can help to cultivate resilience and self-compassion, both of which are vital in overcoming perfectionist tendencies.

In general, being self-aware plays a vital role in defying conformity and embracing genuineness. By comprehending and embracing your own identity, you can deliberately make choices that harmonise with your personal values and true essence, instead of yielding to societal influences and anticipations. Self-awareness has enabled me to identify and question gender stereotypes, to

---

4   James Clear (2018), *Atomic Habits*, Penguin Random House.

capitalise on my strengths and vulnerabilities and to confront my own predispositions regarding others who embrace their true identities.

While we need both authenticity and conformity to survive, they are two opposing forces that shape our lives in significant ways. While authenticity refers to the degree to which we are true to ourselves, our values and our beliefs, conformity refers to the tendency to adopt the beliefs, behaviours and attitudes of the group or society. The degree to which we make choices that are in line with our own unique identity, rather than conforming to societal norms and expectations, is critical.

Ultimately, the choice between authenticity and conformity is a personal one, and there is no right or wrong answer. However, by embracing authenticity and being true to ourselves, we can live a life that is meaningful, purposeful and fulfilling. As American President John F. Kennedy once said, "Conformity is the jailer of freedom and the enemy of growth".[5] By breaking free from the constraints of conformity and embracing our unique identities, we can unleash our full potential and live a life that is truly our own.

---

5   John F. Kennedy (1961), Address by President John F. Kennedy to the UN General Assembly, 25 September, US Department of State (website). Accessed 20 August 2023, https://2009-2017.state.gov/p/io/potusunga/207241.htm

4

Uncovering Your Values and Beliefs

Activating our authenticity involves embracing and expressing our true selves, aligning our actions with our values and cultivating genuine connections with others. This chapter describes the steps towards better understanding of the true self.

Recognising the influence of external factors on your self-concept

In reviewing my expansive book collection, I noticed that I have collected many books centred on the journey of embracing one's true self and shedding concerns about external judgements. One of the early concepts I learned from reading all these books is the importance of discerning what lies within my control and what does not. It is clear to me that attempting to control others is both futile and unnecessary. Instead, I focus on the realm in which I do have power: my own thoughts and responses to external influences. I have developed a practice of deliberately pausing and taking a breath when I find myself becoming entangled in someone else's expectations. This reminds me to release the expectation of being concerned about others' opinions of me.

A book that stands out as a favourite is one by Mark Manson, *The Subtle Art of Not Giving a F*ck*.[10] I like the central theme of learning to distinguish the influence of external factors yet staying true to oneself. Similar to Dr Russ Harris and Prof Hugh Mackay (see pages 45 and 52), Manson challenged conventional wisdom about happiness and success, emphasising the importance of prioritising our values and embracing personal responsibility. He argued that society bombards us with countless messages about what we should care about, encouraging us to seek external validation and base our self-worth on the opinions of others. However, Manson suggested that true fulfilment comes from focusing on what truly matters to us and letting go of the need for constant approval. This concept is further explored in Chapter 7.

Manson encouraged readers to identify their core values and invest their time and energy in pursuits that align with those values. He stated that "that constant positivity is a form of avoidance, not a valid solution to life's problems – problems which, by the way, if you are choosing the right values and metrics, should be invigorating you and motivating you'.[11] Therefore, it is important to understand how external factors can shape our self-concept and influence our authenticity. It is essential to be aware of the

---

10 Mark Manson (2016), *The Subtle Art of Not Giving a F*ck*, Pan Macmillan.
11 Manson, note 18, page 61.

external forces that influence our values, beliefs and behaviours. By doing so, we can differentiate between our true selves and the parts of us that are influenced by external factors.

The first step is identifying influencing external factors. Some of these may include our culture, family members, friends, media and societal norms. They can influence our beliefs, values and behaviours from a young age and may continue to do so throughout our lives.

Growing up under the influence of a strict father, I was raised to prioritise discipline, obedience and respect for authority figures and elders. These values became deeply ingrained in my character and continue to shape my identity today. They were further enforced during my time in the military. It is no surprise that my upbringing and long career in the military shaped some of my values and beliefs.

Adding to this, societal norms regarding gender identity and career expectations have had a significant effect on how I perceive myself. As a woman working in an industry dominated by men, I have faced numerous challenges that have shaped my self-concept and influenced how I view my own capabilities. Early in my life and career, it created much mental torment.

In the early stages of my career in the military, I found myself overexerting myself and going above and beyond the requirements of my role, thereby attempting to prove myself worthy. Eventually I realised that my efforts were futile in changing others' opinions and beliefs about me. It dawned on me that I could only control my own thoughts and behaviours, not the thoughts and perceptions of others. This realisation was liberating. It allowed me to fully comprehend and embrace the unique value I brought to the table, irrespective of others' judgements. I no longer allow others' opinions to dictate how I feel or behave. Instead, I embrace my authentic self and focus on my intrinsic worth and the value I can add. Overall, I feel that it has made me stronger, more resilient and less likely to worry about what others think of me.

However, it is essential to acknowledge that external factors do not have complete control over who we are. Recognising that external circumstances don't entirely shape us is vital when uncovering our values and beliefs. It empowers personal growth, resilience, and responsibility, ultimately leading to a more authentic and fulfilling life journey.

We have the power to choose authenticity and live in alignment with our own values and beliefs. One effective way to achieve this is through self-reflection, whereby we examine our values and beliefs and evaluate how they manifest in our actions and behaviours. An example where I learned the hard lesson of self-reflection was regarding my style of parenting. I did not want my daughters to perceive me in the same light as I had my own father. I understood that my father's upbringing and life experiences influenced his approach to parenting. However, I was determined not to repeat the same patterns. Having experienced the at times negative effects of his parenting on my self-worth and self-esteem, I made a firm commitment to be a better parent.

Yet, I must admit that I have not always gotten it right. For a significant portion of my daughters' younger lives, I remained under the influence of external factors that clouded my judgement and hindered me from being the best parent I could be. Since embarking on my own transformative journey, I now consciously assess the external factors that may be influencing my decisions when interacting with my daughters.

Acknowledging these external influences has empowered me to critically assess their influence and conscientiously make choices that are in harmony with my values and aspirations as a parent. This process, rooted in self-awareness and a desire for continuous growth, grants me a clear perspective that that I can navigate the complexities of parenthood while ensuring that my daughters' wellbeing and growth take precedence.

An illuminating moment occurred while I was on a cruise in 2012, when I had the privilege of meeting Dr Wayne Dyer in person. It was so profound that I still remember what I was wearing at the time and how I felt in his presence. I chose to embark on this cruise with my two young daughters and a friend, motivated by my desire learn more about Dr Dyer's teachings. During a seminar he shared insights from his own journey as a parent, emphasising that the role of a parent is akin to that of a guide who eventually steps back, allowing their children to forge their own path with age-appropriate autonomy. This revelation resonated deeply with me, underlining the importance of imparting wisdom about choice, responsibility and consequences, while respecting my children's individual viewpoints. Embracing this profound lesson, though challenging, has proved indispensable in my parenting journey.

Metaphorically, discovering the influence of external factors on our self-concept is like peeling an onion. As we peel away the layers of external influences, we get closer to our authentic selves.

It can be a challenging process and it can sometimes make you cry, but it is worth the effort to live a fulfilling and purposeful life.

The benefits of self-reflection

Self-reflection involves taking the time to think about your experiences, emotions and behaviours in a non-judgemental way. It enables you to gain insight into your strengths, weaknesses, values and beliefs. Self-reflection is akin to wiping away the dust that obscures the mirror of self-awareness. Much like gazing into a mirror reveals our external appearance, engaging in self-reflection unveils the essence of our inner selves. When our self-perception is clouded by the dust of false images, we lack a genuine understanding of our identity. By meticulously removing this dust, we uncover a clearer, truer reflection of who we are. This unblemished reflection provides a thoughtful comprehension of our character, strengths, values and convictions, empowering us to stand on a foundation of genuine self-appreciation.

I have learned that self-reflection is a critical component of personal and professional growth. In a fast-paced and high-pressure environment, it can be easy to get caught up in the day-to-day tasks and forget to take a step back and evaluate our actions, decisions and goals. However, without self-reflection, we risk becoming stagnant in our development and straying from our true selves. When we take the time to reflect on our experiences, we gain valuable insights into our selves. We can identify areas for improvement and make intentional decisions that align with our goals and values. This, in turn, helps us stay true to ourselves and to live authentically.

One of the benefits of self-reflection is increased cognisance. By examining our thoughts, emotions and behaviours, we can better understand why we react to certain situations in a particular way. This awareness helps us to take ownership of our actions and reactions, rather than being at the mercy of external circumstances. It empowers us to make conscious choices that align with our values, rather than simply reacting to the world around us.

Another benefit is enhanced problem-solving skills. When we take the time to reflect on a problem, we can approach it with a clear mind and an open perspective. This encourages us to consider multiple solutions and identify potential roadblocks. It also helps us to evaluate the pros and cons of each option, ensuring we make the best decision for the situation at hand.

Self-reflection can be challenging. It requires us to be honest with ourselves, which can be uncomfortable and confronting at times. It also requires us to slow down and "be present", which can be difficult in a fast-paced environment.

MY OWN SELF-REFLECTION JOURNEY
Joining the Navy

After 12 years in the military, I reflected on my decision to join the Navy at the age of 18. At this point in my naval career I was contemplating the idea of pursuing a career outside the military. As I reflected on my choices, I realised that before meeting my then husband, I had not encountered anyone with a military background. Surprisingly, my initial career choice was to become an accountant. I excelled in mathematics during my secondary school years and found great enjoyment in it. However, circumstances took an unexpected turn when I was forced to leave home at the age of 15.

Navigating a world of independent decision-making and self-guided learning in the absence of parental guidance proved challenging. My youthful optimism led me to overestimate my maturity. This bravado led to a series of misguided choices, fuelled by a lack of belief in my ability to handle things on my own. At the age of 18, the suggestion to enlist in the military was laid before me: a proposition I embraced without truly understanding the potential magnitude of that decision or how it might irrevocably alter my life's course.

In retrospect, the wisdom of this choice stands in stark contrast to its immediate allure. Adrift in a sea of uncertainty, I lacked not only established guidelines and personal boundaries but also a clear sense of purpose. I found myself akin to a sailing vessel with a fractured mast, meandering at the mercy of external whims and notions, typically divergent from my own.

This reflection highlights the importance of self-awareness and the potential consequences of decisions, even when made with good intentions. It also serves as a reminder of the value of learning from naivety and embracing growth. Engaging in a process of self-reflection provided me with valuable insights into my motivations and the reasons behind my actions. At the time, my choices seemed logical and sensible, but looking back I can understand that I lacked the maturity to fully grasp the consequences that lay ahead. It is likely that this immaturity played a significant role in the ultimate breakdown of my first marriage.

Although my choice to join the Navy has provided me with valuable lessons and personal growth, I often find myself contemplating where I would be today if I had stayed true to myself and pursued my initial ambition of becoming an accountant. I was able to reflect through journalling, at the suggestion of my counsellor, and this facilitated deeper self-reflection on this very matter.

Recording our thoughts and experiences is a good way to gain clarity through self-reflection. Writing enables us to attain a clear understanding and deep insights into our actions and decisions. Seeking feedback from trusted mentors or peers can also offer valuable perspectives, helping us uncover "blind spots" in our thinking or behaviour. It is important, however, to remember that such feedback and advice are external viewpoints and should be considered with the understanding that it is only their perception of us. While well-intentioned advice can be helpful, it is essential to concede that others only know the parts of ourselves that we choose to reveal to the world. They lack intimate understanding of the internal thoughts, desires and motivations that we may not readily share. Ultimately, it is our own inner strength that enables us to identify and engage in self-reflection, determining the direction we wish to pursue and the goals we want to achieve. Therefore, the power to comprehend ourselves lies within, and we must rely on our introspection to navigate our unique journey.

Discovering our authentic self can be a lifelong journey, but it is an essential one. In my experience as a woman and an engineer working in the military, I have seen firsthand how difficult it can be to stay true to oneself in a high-pressure environment that emphasises conformity and obedience. However, with some intentional reflection and practice, it is possible to uncover our authentic self and live a fulfilling life.

Identifying your core values and beliefs

Your core values are the fundamental principles that guide your life and dictate what is truly important to you. They are the foundation of your beliefs, attitudes and behaviours. Reflect on what values resonate with you and why they are meaningful to you. There are numerous tools and resources available to assess how you think and behave in different situations. A list of reputable sources has been provided in the resources section at the end of this book, where you will find some ideas to assist with this process. A simple way to start identifying your values and beliefs is by asking yourself some key questions, such as:

> What do I stand for?
>
> What motivates me?
>
> What makes me happy?
>
> What do I want to achieve in life?
>
> What are my strengths and weaknesses?
>
> What do I want to be remembered for?

As you seek to answer these questions, you may find that certain themes or values begin to emerge. These values may include integrity, honesty, loyalty, compassion, courage and perseverance. But it is important to note that everyone's values and beliefs are unique to them, and that there is no right or wrong answer.

If you find that you are inclined towards a logical and rational approach, some ways to identify your values include making a list of your priorities in different areas of your life, such as relationships, career, personal growth, health and community involvement. Evaluate what matters most to you in each area and examine any conflicts or overlaps that may arise.

Another way you could find what matters most to you is by conducting value assessments. A range of assessment tools and exercises are available online. These resources often present a series of statements or scenarios for you to rank or evaluate, based on their importance to you. If you are not comfortable doing this by yourself, you can enlist the assistance of a coach who specialises in helping people to identify their core values and beliefs. Alternatively, you could engage in philosophical readings or discussions on topics related to ethics, morality and human values. Read books and articles, or listen to audiobooks and podcasts that explore different philosophical perspectives. Reflecting on the ideas presented can stimulate your thinking and help you develop an understanding of your own values and beliefs.

If you are inclined towards creative and artistic endeavours, you could use visualisation and imagery to picture yourself in different situations or scenarios, to help you identify your values and beliefs. For example, you could close your eyes and visualise a scene in which you wake up each morning feeling a deep sense of purpose and fulfillment. "See" yourself engaging in meaningful work that aligns with your values, surrounded by supportive relationships. Feel the joy and contentment that arises from living a life true to your core beliefs.

Another way to get in touch with your true values and beliefs is to spend time in nature and allow yourself to be fully present in the natural environment. Pay attention to your intuitive responses and the messages you receive from nature. Nature has a way of connecting us to our deeper selves and can serve as a mirror to our values and beliefs. Engaging in activities that evoke strong emotions, such as listening to evocative music, watching emotionally charged movies or reading powerful works of literature can also be helpful. Notice how these experiences make you feel, and reflect on the underlying values and beliefs that are triggered by those emotions.

Once you have identified your core values, it is important to align your actions with them. For example, if honesty is one of your core values, strive to be truthful in your interactions with others, even if it is uncomfortable or difficult. If creativity is important to you, make time for activities that enable you to express yourself creatively, whether it be through art, music, writing or another outlet.

The importance of trusting yourself

It is important to listen to your inner voice and trust your intuition when trying to figure out your true values and beliefs. To learn more about this concept, turn to Chapter 10.

In essence, your inner voice is the quiet voice inside you that speaks your truth. It is often drowned out by the noise of external expectations and societal pressures. By taking the time to listen to your inner voice, you can gain clarity and insight into your own guiding principles. Trusting your intuition means trusting your gut feelings and instincts, even if they go against what others may expect of you.

It can be helpful to seek feedback from trusted friends, family members or colleagues. They may be willing and able to offer insights into your values and beliefs that you may not have considered. Or you may have adopted other people's values and beliefs and thought they were your own. However, it is important to remember that, ultimately, the decision about who you want to be and how you want to live your life is yours alone.

Once you have identified your values and beliefs, it is important to align your actions and decisions with them. Chapter 11 will assist with this. I acknowledge that this can be challenging, especially when faced with situations where your values may be in conflict with the expectations of others. However, staying true to your values and beliefs is essential in living an authentic life.

One way to ensure that you are living in alignment with your values is to regularly assess your actions and decisions. Ask yourself if they are in line with your values and, if not, what changes can you make to ensure that they are? This process of self-reflection and adjustment helps you to continuously move in the direction of your authentic self.

It is important to be patient and kind to yourself as you embark on the journey of discovering your values. It is a process that takes time and effort, but the rewards are well worth it. When you are able to live by your own values, you experience a sense of purpose, fulfillment and joy that cannot be found through conformity or external validation. The philosopher Aristotle is attributed as saying, "Knowing yourself is the beginning of all wisdom." Take the time to discover your values, and let that wisdom guide you towards a fulfilling and purposeful life.

MY OWN SELF-REFLECTION JOURNEY
Identifying my core values

Writing this book has been a reflective process and is an example of aligning my life with my core values and beliefs. It began with the realisation that my career as an engineer was not bringing me true happiness. Despite being a skilled engineer, I discovered that teaching and sharing my wisdom resonated more authentically with who I am at my core.

About 16 years ago, when I was an avionics technician, I felt a growing dissatisfaction with my career. After taking some long-service leave, moving to a new locality and some deep soul-searching, I made the decision to leave the military and pursue a degree in psychology. Some well-meaning advice from my Commanding Officer at that time steered me towards an engineering degree sponsored by the Navy. With the responsibilities of being a single parent, it seemed like a logical choice. I ignored my inner voice and, driven by the external success and validation I sought as a commissioned officer, I promptly withdrew my discharge and enrolled in an engineering degree instead.

I justified my decision by attributing my discontent to previous circumstances of not being able to go to sea as a woman in my employment category, and I convinced myself that this new path would allow me to have a greater influence in the Navy. A warning sign emerged soon afterwards, during my third year at university, but despite these signs, I still did not fully embrace my true calling. It took numerous detours and redirections (which will be uncovered throughout this book) before I finally listened to the voice within. It was then that I embarked on my coaching and mentoring journey, which brings me to the present moment, and writing this book. It serves as a testament to the importance of living in alignment with our values and heeding our inner voice, even in the face of external pressures and expectations.

As my experience demonstrates (see case study on previous page), identifying your values and beliefs is an essential step in discovering your authentic self. It helps to guide you in making decisions and living a fulfilling life. Take the time to reflect on your experiences and answer key questions to help identify your values. Remember to stay true to yourself and align your actions with your values, even in the face of external pressures. Think of yourself as a compass, always pointing in the direction of your true north.

Expressing your true self

In her most recent book, *Untamed*,[12] Glennon Doyle stated that embracing one's true self requires courage, vulnerability and a willingness to let go of the need for external validation. She emphasised the importance of listening to our inner voice, trusting our instincts and making choices that align with our own values and desires, rather than seeking approval or conforming to societal expectations. Doyle urged people to honour their own desires, dreams and intuition, even if it means going against the grain or facing criticism. Only then can we dare greatly to express our true selves and become the best versions of ourselves.

There are several ways in which you can learn to express your true self. The first is to practise self-expression. Find healthy and constructive ways to express yourself. This may include writing, art, music or other creative outlets that enable you to communicate your thoughts, emotions and perspectives. Another way is to surround yourself with supportive people. Seek out

---

12 Glennon Doyle (2020), *Untamed: Stop Pleasing, Start Living*, Vermillion.

relationships and communities that accept and encourage you to be your true self. Surrounding yourself with supportive people who celebrate your authenticity can boost your confidence and sense of belonging.

When you are surrounded by like-minded individuals, you are able to take risks and step outside your comfort zone. Taking calculated risks that align with your true self will help you embrace new opportunities and experiences that empower you to grow and express who you are in a supportive environment. If you find that you are not in a supportive environment, make sure you are able to set firm boundaries. Learn to say no when something does not align with your values or does not serve your wellbeing.

5

Embracing Your Vulnerability and Imperfection

When you are willing to share or expose your vulnerability, you permit yourself to be candid and truthful about your emotions and experiences, even in situations that feel uncomfortable or uncertain.

Embracing discomfort for the sake of being authentic requires courage. It involves wholeheartedly exposing your emotions, sharing your imperfections and fearlessly seeking assistance when required. By embracing vulnerability and your shortcomings, you unlock the opportunity to forge genuine connections with others, enabling them to observe and appreciate your authentic self. This unfiltered and sincere revelation not only nurtures empathy but also fosters authentic bonds of understanding and connection.

As a professional engineer, I have often been asked about how I deal with my own vulnerability and emotional regulation when working in a male-dominated environment. The question is inherently biased because it associates vulnerability and being female with weakness and something to be avoided. However, vulnerability is an essential aspect of authenticity, regardless of gender identity, and plays a crucial role in helping us connect with ourselves and others.

In my personal journey of transformation, I have discovered the incredible power of vulnerability in fostering trust and nurturing strong relationships with my peers. However, I must admit that embracing vulnerability has not always been easy for me. Living as a single parent throughout a significant portion of my military career, I often found myself suppressing my emotions and putting on a brave front. Asking for help was something I considered a sign of weakness, believing that I displayed competence by handling everything on my own.

One experience during my first semester at university further solidified my fear of showing signs of not coping. A well-meaning but controlling senior officer remarked that I should not have been accepted into the military education stream for engineering because of the challenges of balancing motherhood, work and studies. She emphasised her own reliance on support from her husband, insinuating that I would ultimately fail under the weight of my responsibilities. This encounter ingrained in me a determination that I should not show "weakness" and the notion that success in my studies meant refraining from seeking help.

In the first three years of my studies, I managed to maintain this facade of being able to handle it all. Behind closed doors, however, my mental health suffered a steady decline. Looking back, I can now admit that I was functioning as a high-achieving individual with hidden depression. Regrettably, my emotional state affected my relationship with my daughters. I was moody, overly strict and burdened by the weight of my self-imposed expectations. I struggled without familial support, but I was determined not to fail. Eventually, this led to an emotional breakdown during my third year of studies.

Reflecting on this period, I now comprehend the damage caused by neglecting my own wellbeing and that of my family. If I could impart one piece of advice, it would be to prioritise your wellbeing and that of your loved ones over the appearance of being vulnerable or seeking help. I am forever grateful to one of my classmates who saw through my facade and extended a helping hand; with their guidance I found my way back onto a path of recovery and self-care.

Through this experience, I learned that vulnerability is not a weakness, but rather a strength. It takes courage to acknowledge our limitations and ask for support. By embracing vulnerability, we open ourselves to authentic connections and create a healthy environment for ourselves and those we care about. I have learned that by being open and honest with my colleagues, I can build a sense of camaraderie and support that helps us to work together and achieve our objectives.

So, what is vulnerability?

Vulnerability is the quality or state of being exposed to the possibility of harm, emotionally or physically. Being vulnerable means being open and honest about who we are and what we feel, even when it's uncomfortable or scary.

For me, vulnerability is about embracing my imperfections and being willing to share them with others. It's about being authentic, even when it's not easy. When we allow ourselves to be vulnerable, we open ourselves to the possibility of being hurt, but we also create space for meaningful connections and personal growth.

During my formative years, vulnerability was not something I readily embraced. Messages like "Don't cry or I'll give you something to cry about" were instilled in me, and I believed that showing emotions was unacceptable. This mindset was reinforced during my time in the military, where emotional vulnerability was deemed weak in an environment dominated by male peers. Consequently, I developed what I considered a tough exterior, disconnecting emotionally from others. Unfortunately, this had a detrimental effect on all my relationships. I struggled to reveal my softer side to my partners and children, leading to moodiness and an unrelenting pursuit of perfection. People found me intimidating and overbearing, unaware of the emotional depth I harboured.

It was only after leaving the military and embarking on a journey of self-discovery that I realised the damage my aversion to vulnerability was causing. I recognised the need to confront the buried emotions that festered within. I discovered that suppressing my emotions was detrimental to my mental health and wellbeing, and it prevented me from forming deep connections with others. With the guidance of a counsellor, I found the courage to peel off the metaphorical bandages and to confront the traumas of my past. Acknowledging and addressing these experiences enabled me to find healing and discover the transformative power of vulnerability, for the sake of my daughters and myself. It was only when I truly embraced my vulnerability was I able to take charge of my life.

The role of vulnerability in authenticity

Authenticity requires us to expose our vulnerability because it means being true to ourselves, even when it is uncomfortable or scary. When we are not being authentic, we may try to protect ourselves from judgement or rejection. We may hide our true selves behind a mask or pretend to be someone we are not.

Embracing our vulnerability is potentially transformative; a tool that can empower us to conquer fear, forge deep connections, enhance our emotional wellbeing and cultivate resilience. I have witnessed the overwhelming effects of exposing my vulnerability, in both my personal and professional lives. Embracing my vulnerabilities and authentically expressing myself enabled me to lead a more meaningful, purposeful life while positively influencing the world around me.

Embracing vulnerability means allowing ourselves to be seen for who we truly are. It's about being honest about our thoughts and feelings, even when they are not popular or easy to express. When we are vulnerable, we give others permission to be vulnerable too, and we create space for authentic connections to form.

I have learned that vulnerability is especially important in the workplace. It can be challenging to admit when we do not know something or to ask for help, but when we do, we create space for growth and collaboration. It can help us build strong relationships with our colleagues and clients. When we are willing to share our experiences and perspectives, we create opportunities for understanding and connection. By being vulnerable, we also show that we trust and respect others, which can inspire trust and respect in return.

Overcoming a fear of vulnerability

As demonstrated, a fear of rejection, judgement or failure can hold us back from sharing our vulnerability and being authentic. However, it is essential to know that vulnerability is a strength, not a weakness, and that it is okay to be imperfect. It is also important to practise self-compassion and self-care. This involves being kind to ourselves and acknowledging that it is okay to make mistakes or to feel uncomfortable. After all, that is how we learn. It also means we need to set boundaries and take care of ourselves, so we do not burn out or become overwhelmed.

A good way to overcome a fear of vulnerability is through practice. Start slowly, by sharing small things with people you trust and gradually building up to more significant and more vulnerable conversations. By doing so, you will develop confidence in your ability to be vulnerable and authentic.

Being unable to embrace our vulnerability can have a significant effect on our mental health. When we suppress our true feelings and emotions, a sense of isolation, loneliness and detachment can ensue. Forming authentic connections with others becomes challenging, leaving us feeling as though we are perpetually donning masks or hiding behind facades.

Bottling up our emotions can lead to negative emotional states such as anxiety, stress and depression. Managing these emotions becomes increasingly difficult, potentially leading to harmful coping mechanisms, including eating disorders and problematic substance use. This downward spiral intensifies negative emotions and behaviours, ultimately compromising our mental wellbeing.

Avoiding exposure of our vulnerability can erode self-esteem and self-worth. Constantly concealing our authentic selves fosters can lead to feelings of inadequacy and a sense of falling short of societal expectations. This perpetuates negative self-talk and self-doubt, gradually undermining our confidence and self-perception.

Finally, avoiding our vulnerability hampers our ability to navigate stress and adversity. When we disconnect from our true emotions, managing challenging situations becomes arduous. This can result in overwhelming feelings of anxiety and helplessness.

Exploring the benefits of vulnerability

One of the key benefits of vulnerability is that it enables us to be authentic and genuine in our interactions with others. When we let down our guard and share our true thoughts and feelings, we invite others to do the same. This can lead to open and honest communication, which in turn can help us to build strong relationships and connections with those around us.

As an example, when I was working as the safety lead on a complex project in rail, I often had to work closely with teams of engineers, designers and other professionals. As I always say, working in safety is like herding cats. Everyone has their own opinions and wants to head off in their own direction. While I was good at my job, I had to rely on the subject-matter experts to understand the issues and challenges the project faced. In some situations, I felt out of my depth as the rail environment was an unfamiliar context. I wanted to rely on my old ways of projecting an image of invincibility or infallibility, to inspire confidence in my abilities. However, I found that this approach often created a barrier between me and the team, making it harder for us to work effectively together.

Instead, I learned to embrace vulnerability and to share my own struggles and challenges with the team. By doing so, I was able to build trust and rapport and this created a collaborative and supportive working environment. When we are all able to be open and honest with each other about our strengths and weaknesses, we are better equipped to tackle challenges and solve problems together.

Another benefit of embracing our vulnerability is that it can help us to develop empathy and understanding for others. When we share our own experiences and struggles with others, we give them permission to do the same. This can help us to build deep connections and to see things from each other's perspectives, even when we disagree.

For instance, as an engineer, I often find myself in situations where I am the only woman in a group of men. In these situations, it can be easy to feel isolated or misunderstood. However, by sharing my own experiences with other women regarding sexism or discrimination, I have been able to connect with others who have had similar experiences, and to build a sense of solidarity and support.

Ultimately, vulnerability is about being willing to show up and be seen, even when we are not sure how others will react. It is about embracing our imperfections and being willing to take risks and make mistakes. Over my career, especially since leaving the military, I have learned that vulnerability is not a weakness, but a strength. I now have better relationships with my colleagues, clients and family.

Strategies for embracing vulnerability

Often, women working in male-dominated fields face unique challenges, such as imposter syndrome, the feeling of not belonging, or being seen as less competent than their male counterparts. These challenges can be a barrier to embracing vulnerability and being authentic. When we face our flaws and weaknesses with honesty and openness, we can respond with self-care and self-love. When we practise self-compassion, we become more resilient in the face of difficulties, better able to handle stress and setbacks, and more willing to take risks and try new things.

Opening yourself to vulnerability entails surrounding yourself with people who genuinely appreciate and accept you for who you are. Seek out connections built on sincerity, where you can express your thoughts and feelings without pretence. Authentic relationships provide a safe space in which to express your true self and contribute to personal growth. Following are some tips to help you embrace your vulnerability.

Sharing your personal stories and experiences

Openly discuss your journey of overcoming challenges, such as conquering a fear or achieving a significant goal. By sharing the ups and downs, you inspire others to embrace their authenticity. Talk about a moment of vulnerability where you took a risk and allowed yourself to be seen and heard. This can encourage others to do the same and create deeper connections.

Expressing your emotions honestly

Share moments of joy and celebrate accomplishments with genuine enthusiasm. By openly expressing positive emotions, you invite others to share in your happiness and create a positive atmosphere. When facing a difficult situation, be willing to express your fears, sadness or vulnerability. This authenticity encourages others to relate to your struggles and creates a space for empathy and support.

Admitting your mistakes and limitations

Reflect on a mistake you have made, take responsibility for it and explain how you learned and grew from the experience. By being open about your imperfections, you encourage others to embrace their own growth opportunities. Discuss a personal limitation or challenge you face, such as a fear or self-doubt. By acknowledging these limitations, you create an environment in which others feel safe to share their own vulnerabilities and seek support.

Seeking support and asking for help

Share a time when you reached out to someone for guidance or assistance, highlighting the positive effect it had on your growth or wellbeing. By demonstrating the value of seeking support, you encourage others to do the same. Discuss a situation in which you overcame the fear of asking for help, showing how it strengthened your relationships and fostered a sense of collaboration and mutual support.

Setting firm boundaries and communicating your needs

Talk about a time when you communicated your boundaries in a relationship or work setting, expressing your needs and expectations. This demonstrates the importance of self-respect and creates healthier dynamics with others. Share an experience where you openly expressed your preferences or desires, allowing others to see and appreciate your authentic self. By communicating your needs, you empower others to do the same, leading to more meaningful connections.

Practising self-compassion

This means treating yourself with the same kindness, concern and understanding that you would offer to a good friend. It involves acknowledging that everyone makes mistakes and experiences setbacks, and that these experiences are opportunities for growth and learning.

I have found that these strategies have helped me to be more authentic and vulnerable in my professional life. When I make a mistake or encounter a difficult situation, I try to remind myself that it is okay to feel uncertain or scared. I give myself permission to make mistakes and to learn from them, rather than beating myself up or feeling like I have to be perfect all the time.

Learning from feedback

To be vulnerable, you must be open to feedback and constructive criticism. It helps you understand how others perceive you and provides an opportunity for growth. Assess the feedback you receive, integrate what resonates with you and make adjustments as needed while staying true to your core values. By being open to feedback, you invite valuable insights and growth opportunities into your life. Feedback provides an external perspective that can shed light on "blind spots" or aspects of yourself that you may not be fully aware of. It helps you gain a deeper understanding of your actions, choices and behaviours, enabling you to align them more closely with your true self.

One of the most significant lessons I have had to grasp involved understanding how I am perceived by others, particularly my daughters. It is uncomfortable to learn that you might be viewed as bossy, domineering or imposing. Yet, those are labels that I have encountered in the past. I have since adopted the habit of scrutinising my actions to identify what might have led to those perceptions. Admittedly, some people will cast a negative light, regardless. However, when your loved ones, who genuinely wish the best for you, hesitate to communicate openly, it is noteworthy. When you extend an invitation and they share things evoking negativity, it is vital to reflect on these responses. Is it your ego at play, or does it merit genuine attention?

Noticing a recurring description of me by different people (unrelated to one another), I acknowledged that the common thread was me. This realisation prompted me to pause and contemplate my conduct. Today, I readily acknowledge instances where I have appeared stern, patronising or abrupt. I would like to believe that I have cultivated a healthy level of self-awareness and continue to actively monitor behaviours that might be perceived as intimidating or condescending.

Embracing your imperfections

Professor Brené Brown's bestseller, *The Gifts of Imperfection,*[13] explores the journey of embracing our imperfections and living as our authentic selves. Prof Brown challenges the societal pressures of perfectionism and shares valuable insights on vulnerability, self-compassion and courage. She encourages readers to let go of the unrealistic expectations imposed by society and to embrace their authentic selves with compassion and courage.

What this means is that we must be ready to fully accept and appreciate the aspects of our selves that are flawed or imperfect, or fall short of societal standards or expectations. It involves recognising and acknowledging our weaknesses, mistakes and

---

13 Brené Brown (2010), *The Gifts of Imperfection,* Hazelden Publishing, Minnesota, USA

limitations without judgement or self-criticism. Rather than striving for an unattainable ideal of perfection, embracing our imperfections means embracing our humanity and understanding that it is through our flaws that we connect with others and experience growth.

Embracing your imperfections is a transformative journey that involves a shift in mindset and a willingness to embrace your true self, flaws and all. It encompasses various aspects that empower you to live authentically and free yourself from the need for external validation. This is not an easy task. While the first idea of imperfections may surface about physical beauty, one thing I always emphasise to my daughters is that you cannot chose your parents or your genes, so learn to be comfortable in the skin you are in. Embracing your imperfections extends beyond external beauty and can also be applied to academic, artistic and other pursuits.

Furthermore, embracing our imperfections involves adopting a growth mindset. It is about viewing mistakes and failures as opportunities for learning and growth. Think about encountering a challenge in your personal or professional life. Instead of seeing it as a roadblock or a reflection of your worth, you adopt a growth mindset. You see the challenge as an opportunity to learn, develop new skills and overcome obstacles, ultimately leading to personal and professional growth. Embracing a growth mindset empowers you to embrace challenges with resilience and a sense of possibility.

CASE STUDY
The bright side of embracing imperfection

Let's consider the example of Adrian, a student who has always been driven by the desire to achieve perfect grades. Adrian puts immense pressure on himself to excel academically and considers anything less than perfection a failure.

I recognise this behaviour in my younger self, from when I was at school and, to some degree, even when I was at university. When a student constantly compares themself to their peers and feels inadequate whenever they make a mistake or receive a lower grade than expected, they may internalise the belief that their worth and intelligence are solely defined by their academic performance. This can lead to fear of failure and a constant need for external validation.

Embracing our imperfections in the context of academic study involves shifting our mindset from a perfectionistic approach to a growth-oriented one. This enables us to identify that making mistakes and facing academic challenges are vital parts of the learning process. It will help us to understand that true growth and development arise through learning from our failures, seeking help and persisting in the face of setbacks.

As Adrian embraces his imperfections in the academic realm, he opens himself up to the idea of taking risks and exploring new areas of knowledge. He begins to appreciate the *process* of learning rather than fixating on the outcome. Such as mindset will free him from the need for constant external validation and will enable him to cultivate intrinsic motivation and a genuine love for learning. Embracing imperfections in his academic pursuits can empower Adrian to define success on his own terms. He will recognise that true success is not defined solely by grades or external accolades, but by cultivating joy in learning, personal growth and the fulfilment that comes from pursuing his passions authentically.

As Adrian adopts the growth-oriented mindset, he will become more resilient and adaptable, better equipped to handle academic challenges and setbacks, with the knowledge that these experiences contribute to their overall development. Additionally, through this experience he may come to inspire and support his peers to embrace their own imperfections and a growth mindset, thereby fostering a culture of learning and growth within his academic community.

Through self-reflection and self-compassion, anyone can learn to accept their imperfections and see them as opportunities for growth. Then setbacks and lower grades are viewed as valuable learning experiences rather than reflections of worth. This shift in perspective will enable them to release the fear of failure and instead focus on personal progress and development.

Ultimately, embracing one's imperfections means letting go of the need for external validation. It means finding validation within yourself and defining your own worth. Imagine pursuing a creative endeavour, such as writing, painting or singing, without seeking constant approval or validation from others. You focus on the joy and fulfilment that comes from expressing yourself authentically, rather than relying on external praise or criticism to define your worth. Letting go of external validation liberates you to fully embrace your imperfections, allowing your genuine self to shine.

It is important to understand that being authentic does not mean being perfect, but rather accepting and embracing your unique qualities; to learn from our mistakes and to define our self-worth internally. Learning to embrace imperfection is a journey of self-discovery and growth. Ultimately, celebrating our imperfections become integral parts of our identity.

6

Facing Your Fears

Fear, which is a complex and universal human emotion, plays a crucial role in our lives. It acts as a survival mechanism, alerting us to potential threats and prompting a "fight-or-flight" response. Our bodies undergo physiological changes when fear arises, and these changes prepare us for action.

We acquire fear through our experiences, which shape our performance and perceptions. While fear serves to protect our wellbeing and motivate us to make safer choices, excessive fear can become problematic. It is in this context that the metaphor of "leaving one's comfort zone" gained popularity over the past few decades. Coined by Judith Bardwick in her 1991 book, *Danger in the Comfort Zone*,[14] the term describes the state in which a person may operate within the realm of "anxiety neutrality", relying on familiar actions to maintain a steady level

---

14 Judith Bardwick (1991), *Danger in the Comfort Zone*, AMACOM.

of performance without taking risks. It highlights the need to confront our fears and embrace discomfort, to achieve personal growth and authenticity.

Remaining in our comfort zone often hinders progress and limits achievement. However, the concept of staying in one's comfort zone can be traced back to the field of behavioural psychology, exemplified by the Yerkes-Dodson Law established in 1908.[15] This law demonstrates the correlation between anxiety and performance, applicable not only to tangible tasks but also to self-understanding and interpersonal relationships. It suggests that our nervous systems have an optimal level of arousal, often referred to as the "Goldilocks zone". Insufficient arousal (or engagement) leads to boredom within the comfort zone, while excessive arousal puts the individual in a state of panic, thereby hindering progress. Stepping beyond our comfort zone requires us to face our fears. When leaving our comfort zone, experiencing fear does not necessarily mean we have entered a zone of panic. Fear can serve as a necessary step towards entering the zones of learning and growth in which personal development, authenticity and fulfillment await (see Figure 2).

---

15 Robert M. Yerkes and John Dillingham Dodson (1908), The relation of strength of stimulus to rapidity of habit-formation, *Journal of Comparative Neurology & Psychology*, *18*(5), 459–482. https://doi.org/10.1002/cne.920180503

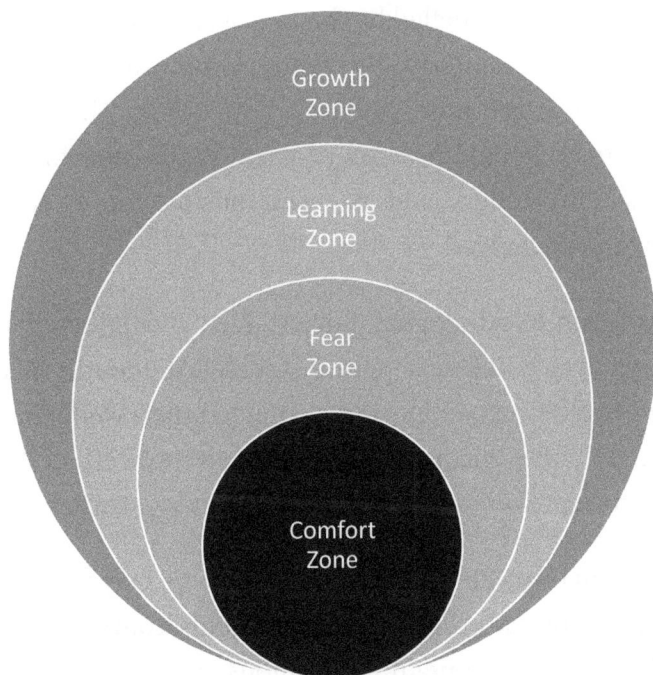

Figure 2: The Comfort Zone[16]

Stepping outside of one's comfort zone can be a daunting prospect for some. The fear associated with leaving the familiar can prevent us from living our most authentic lives, hindering us in the pursuit of speaking genuinely.

Social media has played a significant role in amplifying this fear, giving rise to the phenomenon known as FoMO (fear of missing out). Coined by marketing strategist Dan Herman in 2000,[17] FoMO has gained recognition as a significant psychological and

---

16 Original source of figure unknown. Adapted from various sources provided through the internet

17 Dan Herman (2000), Introducing short-term brands: A new branding tool for a new consumer reality. *Journal of Brand Management, 7*, 330–340. https://doi.org/10.1057/bm.2000.23

social phenomenon, fuelled by the rise of social media and digital connectivity. It manifests differently among individuals, with some experiencing it more intensely than others. The experience of FoMO may include feelings of anxiety, pressure to compare ourselves with others and the compulsion to be constantly connected and engaged.

The Australian Psychological Society (APS) conducted a series of surveys over a five-year period, seeking to identify what was causing people stress and how this affected their wellbeing.[18] Not surprisingly, social media was found to have exacerbated FoMO, which in turn prevented people from being their authentic selves.

In our pursuit of acceptance and validation, we may find ourselves attempting to please others. This desire stems from a genuine need to be liked and to maintain harmonious connections. However, people-pleasing can have detrimental effects on our wellbeing and authenticity. By prioritising others' needs over our own and seeking constant validation, we risk neglecting our own desires and suppressing our true selves.

The fear of not being accepted by others can have a detrimental effect on our mental wellbeing and can hinder our ability to live in alignment with our values and beliefs. This fear commonly arises from a deep-seated need for belonging and connection, since humans are social beings by nature. Fear of rejection or disapproval, can cause significant psychological distress and can lead to a range of negative outcomes. It can lead to a state of

---

18 APS (2015), *Stress & Wellbeing: How Australians are coping with life*. Accessed 7 September 2023, https://psychology.org.au/getmedia/ae32e645-a4f0-4f7c-b3ce-dfd83237c281/stress-wellbeing-survey.pdf

persistent anxiety and self-doubt. We may second-guess ourselves, constantly seeking external validation to confirm our worthiness. This persistent worry about being accepted can consume our thoughts and undermine our self-confidence, thereby eroding our general mental wellbeing.

Moreover, a fear of not being accepted can result in a disconnection from our true selves. To fit in and be liked, we may compromise our values, beliefs and authentic expression. The disconnect between who we truly are and who we feel pressured to be can cause significant internal turmoil and a loss of self-identity. It can lead to feelings of emptiness and confusion, and even self-betrayal.

Furthermore, FoMO or fear of not being accepted can prevent us from pursuing our passions and living authentically. We may do things that we are not comfortable doing, or we may hold ourselves back from taking risks or pursuing our true aspirations, fearing that they might not align with societal expectations or gain approval from others. These fears can hinder our personal growth and limit our potential for fulfilment and success. It can also result in a constant need to please others, and a state of perpetual self-neglect. We may prioritise others needs and desires over our own, sacrificing our wellbeing and personal boundaries in the process. Such self-sacrifice can lead to feelings of resentment, burnout and a diminished sense of self-worth.

However, by embracing our fears and stepping out of our comfort zones, we can initiate a transformative journey of self-discovery that propels us into the learning zone. This zone offers opportunities for personal growth, acquisition of new skills and a broadening of our horizons. By venturing beyond what is familiar, we expose ourselves to different perspectives, cultures and challenges that stimulate our development.

As we extend our comfort zone, we push boundaries and embrace discomfort as a catalyst for progress. Challenges and problems become opportunities for learning and innovation, thereby fostering resilience and adaptability. The journey of self-discovery leads us into the growth zone, where we uncover our purpose, live our dreams and set new goals that are aligned with our passions and aspirations. In this way, we continue to evolve, unlocking our full potential to live a fulfilling and purpose-driven life. We break free from the fear that hinders authenticity, and we embrace the transformative power of stepping outside our comfort zone.

Understanding the role of fear

If we are driven by fear and an inherent desire for authenticity, we may find ourselves yearning to blend in, subtly adjusting our conduct to align with what we believe others might find appealing. However, this seemingly well-intentioned quest for acceptance can have a corrosive effect on our cherished values and deeply held convictions. Fear, typically viewed as a hindrance to our aspirations and dreams, has the potential to serve as a potent catalyst for embracing our genuine selves.

Author and media commentator Arianna Huffington wrote of the transformative nature of fear, on the premise that fear is not the enemy but rather a signal to do something.[19] Throughout my personal coaching journey, I too have discovered the value

---

19 Arianna Huffington (2014), *Thrive*, Penguin Random House.

in perceiving fear as a motivational force that can propel us beyond our comfort zones. One effective strategy I learnt from my coaching studies is to envision fear as an acronym: *False Evidence Appearing Real (FEAR)*. I'm uncertain about the term's originator, but I believe it aptly captures how we should look at our fear response. This perspective stems from the understanding that, often, we fabricate excuses to justify our reluctance. Rarely do genuine and imminent threats to our wellbeing truly exist. By reframing our understanding of fear, we can harness its power to drive meaningful growth and progress.

We also must understand that fear is a natural human response to uncertainty and change. When we step outside of our comfort zone and challenge ourselves to be authentic, we may encounter fears related to rejection, failure or criticism. These fears can be paralysing and may prevent us from taking the necessary steps towards our authentic selves.

However, as noted, fear can also be a valuable signal that we are moving in the right direction. When we feel fear, it often means that we are on the brink of something new and exciting; something that can bring us closer to our true selves. In fact, many successful people attribute their accomplishments to their ability to embrace fear and use it as a motivator.

To use fear as a tool to help us align with our authentic selves, it is important first to identify our fears and understand their root causes. For example, if we are afraid of rejection, we may need to explore the beliefs and experiences that have contributed to this fear. Once we understand our fears, we can begin to take small steps towards our authentic selves, gradually moving into our learning zone.

It is helpful to reframe negative self-talk and focus on strengths and values. When we focus on our strengths and values, we build self-confidence and resilience, which can help us overcome our fears and align with our authentic selves.

Fear is a natural human response to uncertainty and change, and it can be a powerful tool to help us align with our authentic selves. By recognising our fears, moving into our learning zone and reframing our negative self-talk, we can use fear as a motivator to expand our comfort zone and discover new aspects of ourselves. As an engineer working in the military, I learned that embracing fear is essential for personal growth and alignment with authenticity.

Obstacles that fuel FEAR

Before we can tackle FEAR, we need to identify the obstacles that can get in the way, including:

Fear of rejection: Many people fear that if they show their true selves they will be rejected. This can prevent them from being authentic and cause them to conform to the expectations of others.

Fear of vulnerability: Being authentic requires vulnerability. People who are afraid of being vulnerable are concerned that that if they show their true selves they will be judged or rejected.

Social and cultural norms: These social pressures also act as obstacles that fuel FEAR. They dictate how people should behave so that they conform to social expectations.

Personal insecurities: These include low self-esteem, self-doubt and lack of self-confidence; they can prevent people from doing what they truly want to do because they are afraid that their true self is not good enough or may be judged by others, so they suppress their personal beliefs to please others.

Fear of failure: Many people fear failure, for myriad reasons, including some listed here. I like to reframe FAILURE as a First Attempt In Learning – Understanding Realistic Expectations.

Fear of success: Some people can impede growth by causing anxiety over increased responsibilities and expectations, leading to self-sabotage and missed opportunities for personal development.

If we want to live an authentic life, it is important to identify these obstacles and work towards overcoming them. By doing so, you can experience the benefits of authenticity and live a fulfilling life in which you are true to yourself.

Strategies for overcoming fear

Fear can hold us back from showing our true selves, speaking our minds or pursuing our passions. However, with the right strategies, we can learn to overcome our fears and live more authentically.

Reframing negative self-talk

Often, we are our own worst critics, and we may be telling ourselves negative stories about why we cannot be authentic. For example, we may be telling ourselves that we are not good enough, that we do not deserve to be happy, or that we will be rejected if we show our true selves. However, these stories are often not based in reality, and they can hold us back from being authentic.

To reframe, it is important to identify the thoughts that are holding us back and to challenge them. Ask yourself whether these thoughts are really true, or whether they are just stories that you are telling yourself. For example, if you are telling yourself that you are not good enough to pursue your dream job, challenge that thought by asking yourself what evidence you have to support that belief. You may find that the evidence is weak, and that you are basing your beliefs on fear rather than reality.

An example of negative self-talk that is commonly discussed these days is imposter syndrome. Imposter syndrome was first described by Suzanne Imes and Pauline Rose Clance as an observation first among successful women and other marginalised groups. [20] Imposter syndrome refers to a psychological phenomenon whereby individuals doubt their abilities, accomplishments and competence, despite evidence to the contrary. People experiencing imposter syndrome often say they feel like frauds or imposters, fearing that they will be exposed as inadequate or unworthy of their achievements. They may attribute their success to luck or external factors rather than recognising their own skills, qualifications and achievements.

Imposter syndrome has undeniably cast its shadow over my life, its roots tracing back to the damaging effects of childhood trauma

---

20 Pauline R. Clance and Suzanne A. Imes (1978), The imposter phenomenon in high achieving women: Dynamics and therapeutic intervention. *Psychotherapy: Theory, Research & Practice,*15(3):241–7. https://doi.org/10.1037/h0086006

and the hurtful words inflicted by my father. Slowly but surely, I internalised those damaging voices, allowing them to shape my perception of self. It sometimes bewildered me how others perceived me as confident, self-assured and driven, when I was all too aware of my internal struggles. It has taken years of unwavering commitment to reframe my internal narrative.

A pivotal moment was when I confronted the toxic relationships that perpetuated this cycle of self-doubt and negative self-talk. Summoning courage, I scrutinised my circle of friends and identify those whose presence posed a threat to my wellbeing. Over time I distanced myself from these individuals and sought connections with like-minded souls who shared my values and beliefs. This process proved challenging, and to this day I remain vigilant in assessing the influences that surround me.

In addition to evaluating my relationships, I embarked on a soul-searching journey regarding my career choices. While I had been praised for being a skilled engineer, I realised that my true passion did not align with that profession. With a resolute spirit, I took deliberate steps to redirect my career. Though I continue to find joy in teaching and sharing my engineering knowledge, my realignment with my true self enabled me to embrace new roles as a coach, mentor and teacher.

Over time, I have learned that overcoming imposter syndrome necessitates continuing self-reflection. In doing so I take ownership of my self-talk and make deliberate choices about the people I surround myself with. Each small step has contributed to my personal growth and has empowered me to embrace my true worth and capabilities.

Setting boundaries

Overcoming fear can be achieved through the power of small steps towards authenticity. The prospect of making substantial life alterations, such as changing careers or terminating relationships, can be daunting. People often delude themselves with the notion of "better the devil you know" and remain trapped in fear's grip. However, by breaking down the process into manageable increments, we can build momentum and embrace our true selves.

These small steps may involve setting boundaries with unsupportive individuals in our lives, exploring new hobbies or activities that resonate with our authentic selves, or expressing our genuine emotions in a safe and nurturing environment. By taking these small strides, we gradually cultivate confidence and establish a positive trajectory towards living a more authentic life.

Imagine yourself attending a casual social gathering with a group of acquaintances. In the past, you may have felt compelled to hide certain aspects of your personality to "fit in" and avoid judgement. However, now you are determined to break free from this pattern and embrace your true self. Within this relaxed context, you initiate a conversation by openly sharing your sincere viewpoints on casual subjects like movies or hobbies. You express your genuine thoughts and inclinations, even if they veer from the mainstream. As you observe the encouraging reactions and active participation from others, you realise that your authenticity not only finds acceptance but is genuinely valued. If the responses are not positive, reflect on your core values and the company you keep. Do they harmonise? If not, perhaps distancing yourself from such individuals may be a wise course of action.

If you are encouraged by this experience, take another small step by sharing a personal anecdote or story that reflects your true values and experiences. This vulnerability will invite deeper connections and genuine conversations with those around you.

By consistently practising the setting of boundaries in these less intimidating situations, you gradually nurture a sense of confidence and witness the positive outcomes it brings. Each small victory serves as a building block, reinforcing your belief in the value of staying true to yourself.

Over time and with practice, you can extend this authenticity to more challenging circumstances, such as professional settings or close relationships. The confidence and positive experiences gained from your initial small steps provide a solid foundation, and can empower you to navigate these situations with increased authenticity and self-assurance.

Creating supportive networks

Fear can be a significant obstacle when it comes to embracing authenticity. It is essential to remember that authenticity is not the same as perfection. When making changes in your life, it is natural to experience fear and uncertainty, and it is okay to make mistakes along the way. In fact, vulnerability and authenticity often go hand in hand; being willing to show your imperfections can deepen connections with others.

Therefore, an effective strategy for overcoming fear is to seek out a supportive community. Surrounding yourself with people who accept and support you in your endeavours can be incredibly empowering. This community may consist of friends, family members or like-minded colleagues and acquaintances who share your values and aspirations. Being part of a supportive community can help to alleviate feelings of isolation on your journey and can provide the encouragement and motivation needed to persevere.

Seeking professional assistance

In addition to seeking support from friends and family, it can be beneficial to seek guidance from a coach or mentor. These professionals provide a future-focused perspective and offer strategies and techniques to navigate your fears and develop a stronger sense of authenticity. Through coaching, you can explore the underlying causes of your fears, set realistic goals to overcome your fears and build resilience.

Another way you can grow as a person is to seek guidance from professionals who specialise in cognitive-behavioural therapy (CBT), mindfulness, or exposure therapy can provide valuable techniques to confront and overcome fear. These approaches can help you develop resilience, change in negative thought patterns, and build emotional strategies, ultimately enabling you to navigate challenges and achieve personal growth more effectively.

By seeking support from trusted individuals, whether they are friends, family or professionals, you can alleviate the weight of fear and gain valuable insights and encouragement. The empathetic listening, understanding and guidance provided by these people will empower you to confront your fears, embrace authenticity and continue growing on your personal journey.

Final words on overcoming fear to become your authentic self

Overcoming fear is often associated with stepping out of the darkness and into the light. Fear can keep people confined in their comfort zones and overshadowed with doubt. By summoning the strength to confront their fears, we can step into the light of self-discovery, growth and empowerment.

To preserve our mental wellbeing and live in alignment with our values and beliefs, it is crucial to address and overcome the fear of not being accepted. This involves cultivating self-acceptance and self-compassion, accepting that our worth is not determined by others' opinions. It also requires us to surround ourselves with supportive and accepting people who appreciate us for who we truly are. By prioritising our own values, pursuing our passions and embracing our authentic selves, we can foster a sense of fulfilment, resilience and mental wellbeing.

While fear can serve as a protective mechanism, it can also become irrational or disproportionate in certain situations. It is important to note that fear is a normal and necessary aspect of human existence. It alerts us to potential dangers and helps us make decisions that ensure our safety and wellbeing.

However, excessive or irrational fear can hinder personal growth, limit opportunities and negatively affect mental health. Understanding and managing fear, using techniques provided by supportive professionals, such as cognitive-behavioural therapy, mindfulness or exposure therapy, can empower individuals to overcome their fears and lead fulfilling lives.

7

Breaking Free from Society's Expectations

Almost from the moment we are born, we are encounter societal expectations that play a role in shaping our lives and choices. We are told how to behave, what to wear, what to study and what careers to pursue. Unfortunately, these expectations can limit our true potential and hinder our ability to express our authentic selves. As we grow older, these societal pressures become even more pronounced, particularly in the workplace.

For women in male-dominated fields such as engineering, aviation and other related STEM (science, technology, engineering, mathematics) fields, the weight of having to conform to societal norms can be overwhelming, and can perpetuating a cycle of self-doubt and stifled ambition. In this chapter, we embark on a transformative exploration of societal expectations and their effects on women in STEM, to find out how to overcome these barriers.

The chapter describes the unique challenges faced by women in STEM and offers strategies for breaking free from the confines of conformity. The aim is to empower women to embrace their authenticity and to thrive in the STEM world, on their own terms. By embracing our true identities, questioning societal norms and making choices that align with our values and aspirations, we can forge a path that celebrates our uniqueness, cultivates personal fulfilment and defies the limitations imposed by a conformist society.

Gender identity and societal expectations

Biases and stereotypes on the basis of gender identity are prevalent in STEM fields and can create obstacles to attracting girls and women to STEM studies and careers, and later can hinder their retention and progression in these studies and careers. Australian society has long perpetuated the myth that engineering is field best suited to men, and this has resulted in a lack of female representation in engineering industries. Historically, the profession of engineering has been dominated numerically and intellectually by men in Australia and many other countries.

According to Engineers Australia's 2019 Statistical Report, participation of women in the engineering profession grew by 112.4 per cent between 2006 and 2016.[21] However, the proportion of women in the profession remained relatively small, at 13.6

---

21 Engineers Australia (2019), Statistics (webpage, last updated 22 October 2022). Accessed 11 September 2023, https://www.engineersaustralia.org.au/about-engineering/statistics

per cent in 2016. The report cited university statistics for 2020, indicating that women commencing engineering courses increased to 18 per cent.

In military aviation, where I began my career, the statistics are less encouraging. Women make up around 10 per cent of the Australian pilot community and 15 per cent of Royal Australian Air Force (RAAF) staff. In 2021 there were just 38 female pilots in the RAAF, representing 5 per cent of the 752 pilots in the air force and 2 per cent of Australia's aeronautical engineers were women.[22]

In 2022, the Australian Department of Industry, Science and Resources identified that women made up 36 per cent of enrolments in university STEM courses, and 16 per cent of enrolments in vocational STEM courses.[23] Women made up 27 per cent of the workforce across all STEM industries, a one percentage point drop from 2020. In STEM-qualified industries, 23 per cent of senior management and 8 per cent of CEOs in were women.

It is worth noting that these statistics may have changed since their publication, given recent initiatives to promote diversity and inclusion in the engineering disciplines and in STEM more broadly. However, the lack of gender diversity can contribute a

---

22 Hannah Dowling (2021), The fight for flight and addressing female under-representation in aviation, *Australian Aviation Magazine, Issue 381.* Accessed 20 August 2023, https://australianaviation.com.au/2021/08/feature-the-fight-for-flight-and-addressing-female-under-representation-in-aviation/

23 Department of Industry, Science and Resources (2022), The state of STEM gender equity in 2022 (webpage, updated 23 September). Accessed 11 September 2023, https://www.industry.gov.au/news/state-stem-gender-equity-2022#:~:text=Women%20only%20make%20up%2036,STEM%2Dqualified%20industries%20are%20women.

culture that is not welcoming to women, and can make it difficult for women to feel like they do not belong.

Underrepresentation of women in STEM courses indicates a lack of encouragement and support for women and girls to pursue these fields of study. This may be due to societal biases, gender stereotypes and limited access to resources and opportunities, which not only restricts the personal and professional growth of women but also hampers the potential for diverse perspectives and contributions in STEM disciplines.

Furthermore, the low representation of women in the STEM workforce, especially in senior management and leadership positions, indicates suggests there may be significant barriers and biases that hinder women's career progression in the sector. In turn, this lack of representation leads to limited role models and mentorship opportunities for women and girls, making it more challenging for them to envision thriving and advancing within STEM industries. It also perpetuates a cycle of limited diversity, thereby influencing decision-making processes, innovation and the overall inclusivity of the STEM sector.

The underrepresentation of women in STEM fields reflects the influence of societal expectations and poses challenges for women to break free and be authentic in a conformist world. It highlights the need for women to overcome the biases and barriers that limit their opportunities to express their authentic selves and pursue non-traditional careers.

Merryn McKinnon, a researcher at the Centre for the Public Awareness of Science, Australian National University, and Christine O'Connell, from the School of Journalism, Stony Brook

University in the United States, identified that the awareness of being negatively perceived, or feeling like an "other" can have a significant effect on one's identity, whether it relates to a specific gender identity or being someone involved in scientific pursuits.[24] They cite previous studies indicating that people from marginalised groups may even further penalise those who display traits associated with their marginalised identities. Consequently, people from marginalised groups may hesitate to exhibit these identity traits, undermining efforts to promote workplace diversity and inclusion. For instance, research has shown that women in academia are often evaluated on the basis of their personality rather than their abilities, in contrast to their male counterparts. Women are expected to exhibit nurturing and empathetic qualities. These stereotypes have implications for women's careers if they do not conform to the "warm" stereotype, but they can also penalise other women who exhibit such stereotypical demeanours. Additionally, accomplishments that challenge the stereotypes, such as women excelling in scientific fields, are often discounted or attributed to external factors.

The pressure to conform to societal expectations can be particularly acute for women engineers, who may be expected to behave in ways that are considered "traditionally feminine", such as being nurturing and empathetic, rather than assertive and decisive. Women engineers may feel they need to suppress certain aspects of their personality to fit in.

---

24 Merryn McKinnon and Christine O'Connell (2020), Perceptions of stereotypes applied to women who publicly communicate their STEM work, *Humanities and Social Sciences Communications*, 7(160), https://doi.org/10.1057/s41599-020-00654-0_

By addressing the gender disparity in STEM and promoting inclusivity, we can create an environment that supports women in pursuing their passions authentically. Encouraging women to enter STEM fields, providing mentorship and challenging gender biases will contribute to developing a more diverse and innovative landscape in STEM. Embracing authenticity can enable women to challenge norms, make meaningful choices and contribute their unique perspectives to society.

There are several ways in which women in STEM can break free from society's expectations and move forward in embracing our authenticity, including the following.

Challenge limiting beliefs

Embrace the opportunity to challenge and redefine your beliefs about success in your career and the role you take in life. Reflect on whether these beliefs stem from societal expectations or align with your authentic values. If you find that they are rooted in societal expectations, it may be time to reassess and forge a new path towards your unique definition of success. Along this journey, be vigilant in identifying limiting beliefs imposed by society, family or well-meaning others that hinder your authenticity and individualism. It is essential to question the validity of these beliefs and replace them with empowering and affirming thoughts that resonate with your true self. Remember, you have the power to create an uplifting example to follow by boldly defying societal norms, embracing your authenticity and shaping a successful life that is true to your own aspirations and values. Your journey will inspire others and pave the way for a more inclusive and diverse future.

Break the chains of conformity

Engineers are known for their problem-solving abilities and are well-equipped to tackle complex challenges. Breaking free from societal expectations, as an engineer or a woman in STEM requires us to apply those problem-solving skills to break the chains of conformity. We can start by recognising these expectations and the pressure to conform. By identifying these constraints, analysing the situation at hand and thinking innovatively, we can design solutions to liberate us from societal pressures. This process will enable us to challenge expectations, paving the way to embrace our authentic selves. Breaking free from societal expectations starts with a conscious choice to defy conformity, and this opens up a world of self-expression and personal fulfilment. Strategies for doing just that are described here.

Define your own success

Challenge societal definitions of success and chart your own extraordinary path. Look beyond superficial markers like wealth and status, and delve into the depths of your soul to discover what true success means to you. Embrace your unique values and aspirations, allowing them to illuminate the way forward. While the saying, "If you can see it, you can be it," is often repeated in STEM fields these days, I stand as living proof that you can break barriers and blaze trails without having a specific role model. I have defied the limitations of what a woman could achieve without having female role model, and have demonstrated that it is possible to be the guiding light for others even in the absence of examples or role models.

Popular culture and the media have perpetuated a prevalent stereotype of the white male engineer, which has discouraged girls and women from pursuing careers in STEM. In my three decades in the industry, I have witnessed firsthand the lack of female role models and mentors. Jessica Gladstone and Andrei Cimpian carried out studies relating to STEM students and how role models could be used to attract and retain more women and racial/ ethnic minorities to STEM related roles.[25] The research found that role models are important because they inspire and motivate individuals by providing tangible examples of success and character traits to emulate. They can also offer guidance, helping people navigate challenges and make positive life choices. However, I firmly believe that we can overcome these challenges by challenging societal expectations head-on and actively fostering a robust network of female role models and mentors within the aviation industry. Together, we can empower future generations of young women to envision themselves, not just surviving but thriving in the world of aviation, STEM and engineering. Let us inspire them to fearlessly pursue their dreams and shatter the glass ceilings that may stand in their way.

Embrace your unique qualities

Following my departure from the military, acquaintances remarked that they had observed a change in my personality. I find that as I get older and wiser, my commitment to self-improvement paves the way for an increasingly authentic version of myself.

---

25 Jessica Gladstone and Andrei Cimpian (2021), Which role models are effective for which students? A systematic review and four recommendations for maximizing the effectiveness of role models in STEM, *International Journal of STEM Education, 8(59)*. https://doi.org/10.1186/s40594-021-00315-x

This transformative journey has been a gradual undertaking, with few overnight revelations. Yet, I sometimes contemplate how different my life's course might have been if I had cast aside the masks I had donned during the early stages of my career. If I had wholeheartedly embraced my apparent abilities, exhibited a greater degree of vulnerability and fully embraced my identity as a woman, where might this have led me?

Certainly, I have encountered moments of self-doubt and experienced the uneasiness that accompanies the pivotal decisions I have had to make in my life. These feelings, however, are familiar companions. It is commonplace for individuals to magnify their perceived flaws and errors, fixating on areas they believe require "mending" and often neglecting their inherent strengths. This self-critical mindset can contribute to feelings of inadequacy and can hinder the capacity to nurture meaningful connections. Nonetheless, it is crucial to realise that appreciating one's positive attributes holds a distinctly important place alongside acknowledging and gleaning insights from our shortcomings or missteps.

Concerns about appearing arrogant or self-absorbed should not prevent you from valuing your strengths. Even individuals with great humility can have a positive self-perception. They appreciate their strengths without exaggerating them or feeling the need to announce them to the world. Similarly, you can maintain a balanced perspective on your strengths or accomplishments, recognising them as experiences to feel good about while acknowledging that they are part of a humanly imperfect package.

Every person is unique and cannot be someone else. Like a snowflake, you possess distinct characteristics and a personality that sets you apart. As Frida Kahlo aptly expressed, "I am my own muse. I am the subject I know best. The subject I want to know better".[26] Instead of striving to fit into a predetermined mould, embrace your unique qualities and strengths. These qualities are what make you stand out and differentiate you from your peers. They help people identify who you are and appreciate your distinctive abilities.

Seek growth and learning

As you continue your journey of personal growth and lifelong learning, it is essential to embrace diverse strategies that expand your horizons and unveil new facets of yourself. One powerful approach involves actively engaging in activities that spark your interest, even if your initial proficiency seems elusive. It may be necessary to adopt strategies that can broaden your perspective and reveal unexplored dimensions of yourself.

Reflecting on my own life, a powerful example is the choice I made at age 34 to pursue higher education. Not having completed high school, I believed that university study was beyond my grasp. While I briefly pondered a range of study options, I struggled to justify the investment in time and money, especially in the realm of psychology which I was considering.

---

26 Isabella Myer (2021), Frida Kahlo quotes – life lessons from the profound Frida Kahlo (webpage, updated 16 August 2023). Accessed 11 September 2023, https://artincontext.org/frida-kahlo-quotes/

Fortuitously, an encouraging supervisor identified my untapped potential and urged me to chase further education. Despite my reservations and excuses, this mentor emerged as an unwavering advocate, helping me to chart viable routes to success. He supported and encouraged me to sit entrance exams to pinpoint my strengths. He bolstered my confidence, assuring me that my technical background as an aviation technician held promise, that it was possible for me to thrive in engineering. This led me to discard the idea of psychology and embark on an eye-opening expedition into the world of engineering.

Subsequently other areas of my life have improved in significant ways. After I earned a bachelor's degree in engineering, I completed a master's degree in engineering, with a focus on airworthiness. This ignited a passion within me for further study focusing on the human element in aviation. In turn, this prompted me to delve deeper into human behaviour, and I acquired a graduate diploma in human factors. Still unsatisfied, I ventured further to secure a graduate certificate in transport safety investigations and, in line with psychological aspects, a diploma in coaching. This study converged with my zeal for assisting others. They stand as a testament to the transformative might of confronting fear, transcending self-imposed constraints and embarking on a voyage of personal fulfilment and growth.

Venturing into unexplored territories presents invaluable opportunities for learning and self-discovery. Moreover, enrolling in courses that facilitated the acquisition of new knowledge and skills proved to be highly advantageous for me. Such educational pursuits broaden our perspectives and also equip us with essential tools for personal development. Engaging in experiences that foster genuine self-discovery and authentic expression can have a transformative effect. These encounters enable us to explore the different aspects of our identity, challenge preconceived notions and venture beyond the confines of our comfort zone. By embracing these paths, we embark on a continuous journey of growth, expanding our horizons and unearthing latent potential that previously remained untapped within ourselves.

Practise integrity

Integrity is unwavering honesty and moral uprightness; means consistently upholding strong principles and values and involves aligning our actions with our beliefs, even when no one is watching. Integrity fosters trustworthiness, respect and a solid ethical foundation. Therefore, practising integrity to overcome fear can benefits us in several ways. It helps us remain true to our values and principles, guiding our actions and boosting self-confidence. It builds trust in relationships, fostering deep connections and collaboration with those we interact with. Integrity also cultivates resilience and perseverance, by enabling us to overcome challenges and learn from our failures. Having integrity leads to authenticity and purpose, as we make choices aligned with our passions and aspirations.

To reap the benefits of staying true to your values and embracing your fear, it is essential to align your actions with your values. This means being consistent in your words and deeds, so you can build trust and credibility with others. For instance, if honesty is a core value, practising integrity means being truthful even when it is uncomfortable or inconvenient. By doing so, you establish a reputation for reliability and sincerity, strengthening your relationships and creating a sense of trust.

Integrity also reinforces your authenticity and helps you stay true to yourself. When faced with fear, make choices that align with your genuine beliefs and principles. For example, if you value personal growth, pushing past your comfort zone to pursue new experiences or acquire new skills demonstrates integrity in action. By honouring your values, you cultivate a strong sense of self and a genuine connection to your aspirations and purpose.

Practise self-expression

In a conformist world that constantly pressures us to fit into predefined stereotypes, self-expression becomes an act of liberation and authenticity. It is a means of breaking free from societal expectations and embracing our true selves. By finding and nurturing our inner voice, we empower ourselves to transcend the limitations imposed by society and cultivate a deep connection with our authentic desires, beliefs, and aspirations.

... through creative arts

One powerful form of self-expression in the creative arts is through music. Singing or playing an instrument helps us to communicate our emotions and thoughts in ways that may be difficult to express otherwise. Music gives us a platform from which to unleash our innermost feelings, share our stories and connect with others on an emotional level. Whether we sing alone in the shower, perform on stage or jam with friends, music can empower us to break free from conformity and let our unique melodies resonate with the world.

If you are not the singing type, listening to music or partaking in creative movement, such as dancing or exercise, is another potent way you can be creative. Exploring our creativity enables us to communicate through our bodies, thereby releasing energy and emotions through fluid and expressive movements. Dancing offers a way to embrace our physicality, celebrate our individuality and break free from the rigid constraints of societal norms. It empowers us to find freedom in the rhythm and grace of our bodies, forging a connection between our inner selves and the outer world.

... through clothing and dress

Clothing has long been a powerful means of self-expression. It enables us to showcase our personal style, values and identity, serving as a visual representation of our true selves. By dressing authentically, we defy societal expectations and celebrate our uniqueness. It is a statement that we refuse to be confined by conventional norms. The transformation of professional attire has been evident even before the pandemic, but COVID-19 has accelerated this change.

Dr Briony Lipton and her colleague, Sulagna Basu, conducted research confirming that since the start of the COVID-19 pandemic, there has been a notable shift towards more casual fashion choices as people began to work from home and then as they returned to the office environment.[27] They undertook a nationwide survey involving 1155 participants, enquiring about their experiences of preparing for work prior to the pandemic and during this time, and explored participants' perspectives on work attire and professionalism within their respective industries.

Beyond the popular refrain of "business up top and party on the bottom" as appropriate dress when attending meetings online, there are deeper connections to explore between professional appearance, work environment and workplace gender equality. Understanding the gendered effects of remote work on women's careers and the emergence of new workplace cultures influenced by attire and physical location is of utmost importance.

While respondents to the study by Lipton and Basu agreed on the continuing importance of appearance, it is interesting to note that women, more than men, emphasised its role in how they are perceived at work. As the work landscape continues to evolve, let us embrace the power of self-expression through our clothing choices and build a future in which authenticity and diversity are celebrated in every aspect of our professional lives.

... through writing

Writing or journalling is a great tool to help us break free from conformity and to embrace authenticity. Writing is a form of self-expression that transforms abstract emotions and experiences

---

27 Briony Lipton and Sulagna Basu (2022), Covid Casual: Refashioning Professional Work Attire in the Age of Remote Work. The University of Sydney, doi: 10.25910/ 2bwq- pg97. Accessed 11 September 2023, https://ses.library. usyd.edu.au/bitstream/handle/2123/27461/COVID%20Casual%20Report. pdf?sequence=3&isAllowed=y

into tangible and real manifestations. Through the act of writing, we give shape and substance to our thoughts, ideas, experiences and emotions. Writing is the very essence of art itself, the conduit through which our heart and soul find expression. It also provides us with a medium to not only understand ourselves but also to communicate with others. It offers an intimate and introspective outlet whereby we can explore the depths of our inner world. With honesty and vulnerability, we can identify our thoughts, emotions and experiences to gain a deep understanding of who we truly are. Writing enables us to unravel our deepest musings, giving form to our innermost desires, fears and aspirations.

Writing grants us the freedom to authentically express our innermost thoughts and feelings, unrestricted by societal norms or expectations. It empowers us to break free from the confines of conformity and to embrace the power of our authentic voices. Through our words, we untangle ourselves from the grip of conformity, embracing our unique perspectives and experiences.

Whether we choose to keep our writings private as personal reflections, or choose to share them with others, writing gives us the opportunity to be true to ourselves. It enables us to celebrate our individuality, giving voice to our inner truths and experiences. In this process, we affirm our authenticity and honour the uniqueness that sets us apart from the crowd.

The benefits of embracing authenticity in a conformist world

When we have the courage to embrace our authentic selves and break free from societal expectations, we unlock a multitude of benefits that can positively influence our lives. Following are some significant advantages of embracing authenticity.

Increased confidence: Embracing authenticity cultivates a sense of self-assurance and confidence. By honouring our true desires, values and beliefs, we become more self-aware and secure in our abilities and decisions. This newfound confidence empowers us to pursue our goals, take risks and navigate life's challenges with resilience and conviction.

Improved relationships: Authenticity forms the foundation for genuine connections with others. When we show up as our authentic selves, we invite others to do the same. This openness and vulnerability create space for deep, meaningful relationships built on trust, understanding and acceptance. Authenticity enables us to attract and surround ourselves with people who appreciate us for who we truly are, fostering authentic and fulfilling connections.

Greater resilience: Authenticity equips us with the strength to face adversities and bounce back from setbacks. By embracing our true selves, we develop a solid sense of identity and purpose that helps us stay grounded and navigate challenges with resilience. Authenticity empowers us to face difficult situations with integrity, adaptability and the courage to stay true to our values. Ultimately, it leads to personal growth and the ability to overcome obstacles.

Better mental health: Conforming to societal expectations can generate internal conflicts, leading to stress, anxiety and even depression. Embracing authenticity promotes a sense of inner harmony and alignment. By living in alignment with our true selves, we reduce the burden of trying to meet external standards and expectations. This liberation from societal pressures alleviates internal conflict and fosters improved mental wellbeing.

Staying true to yourself while navigating societal norms

The pressure to conform to societal expectations can be overwhelming, especially for women in male-dominated disciplines like STEM. However, by recognising these expectations and embracing our authentic selves, we can break free from the constraints of conformity and create a fulfilling life. As women in non-traditional employment roles, it is important to support each other and challenge the status quo, so that we can create a more diverse and inclusive industry.

My business, Winter & Associates, was established with the aim of providing valuable guidance and support that can truly impact people's lives in a positive way. Our services are not limited to women; they are for anyone who may feel marginalised or excluded, with a special focus on promoting the employment of women in non-traditional roles. Embracing the acronym theme, WINTER represents "Women in Non-Traditional Employment Roles," reflecting our commitment to breaking gender barriers. While it is important to stay true to yourself, it is also important to be open-minded. This means being willing to consider different perspectives and ideas. Being open-minded can help you navigate societal norms in a way that aligns with your values and beliefs, while still being respectful of others' values and beliefs.

Staying true to yourself while navigating societal norms can be challenging, but it is possible. By identifying your values and beliefs, setting boundaries, surrounding yourself with like-minded people, being open-minded and practising self-reflection, you can stay true to yourself while continuing to navigate societal norms. Remember, staying true to yourself is important for your mental health and overall wellbeing.

8

Improving Your
Self-Awareness

Self-awareness, as described in Chapter 2, is a fundamental concept that encompasses an individual's conscious awareness of their internal state and their interactions and relationships with others. If you search online (try Google Scholar for peer-reviewed research findings) for "self-awareness" and "effects on positive psychological wellbeing" you will find many different studies that support the positive outcomes of practising self-awareness techniques.

Interestingly, research conducted by Anna Sutton found that, within the realm of self-awareness, there are two primary categories that can be identified: situational self-awareness and dispositional self-awareness.[28] This is important to note as

28 Anna Sutton (2016). Measuring the effects of self-awareness: Construction of the self-awareness outcomes questionnaire, *European Journal of Psychology*, *12*(4):645–658. doi: 10.5964/ejop.v12i4.1178

situational self-awareness is an automatic process that enables individuals to grasp their surroundings and capabilities, and to compare their actions with their internal standards. It provides insights to guide the individual's adjustments. In contrast, dispositional self-awareness involves an individual's inclination to focus on and contemplate their psychological processes, subjective experiences and relationships with others. It is not the intention of this book to delve into these studies. More so, the intention is to provide perspective and insight as to why self-awareness is important in recognising and embracing your strengths and weaknesses.

I like to view self-awareness as the illuminating mirror that enables us to see ourselves clearly, recognising both our strengths and weaknesses with honesty and compassion. Just as a mirror reflects our physical image, self-awareness provides a reflective space in which we can examine our inner landscape, acknowledging our unique qualities and areas for growth. By embracing self-awareness, we cultivate a deep understanding of ourselves; it empowers us to navigate life with authenticity, resilience and a commitment to personal development.

To illustrate this point, the Johari Window, developed by psychologists Joseph Luft and Harry Ingham in 1955, serves as a valuable tool to enhance self-awareness and foster improved communication within relationships and groups.[29] The Johari Window, as shown in Figure 3, is designed to illustrate the different aspects of knowledge and information within an individual's

---

29 Joseph Luft and Harry Ingham (1955), The Johari window, a graphic model of interpersonal awareness, *Proceedings of the Western Training Laboratory in Group Development*, University of California Los Angeles.

awareness. It consists of four quadrants that represent the various dimensions of self-awareness.

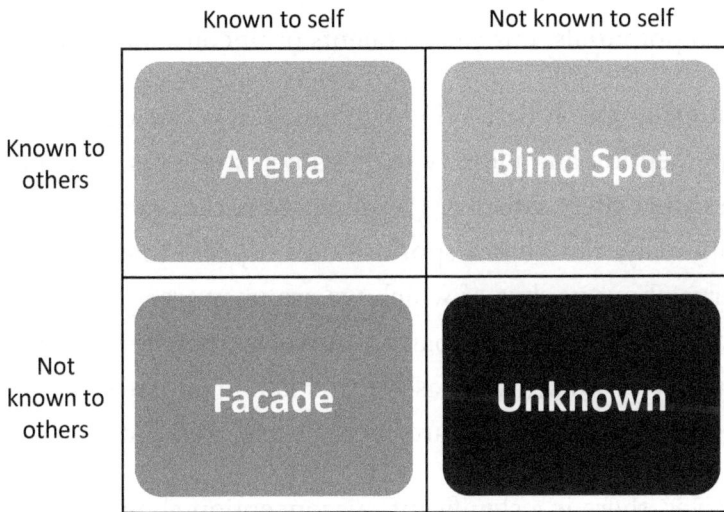

Figure 3: The Johari Window

Arena: This quadrant includes information, behaviours, feelings or thoughts that are known to both the individual and others. It represents the aspects of ourselves that we willingly share with others.

Blind spot: This quadrant represents information or behaviours that others can perceive about us, but we may be unaware of ourselves. It consists of blind spots or aspects of our personality that we may overlook or not recognise.

Façade: This quadrant contains information, feelings or thoughts that are known to the individual but not shared with others. It represents our private thoughts, emotions or experiences that we choose to keep hidden or disclose selectively.

Unknown: This quadrant represents information or behaviours that are unknown to both the individual and others. It encompasses undiscovered aspects of ourselves, including hidden potentials, unrealised talents or unconscious patterns.

By utilising the Johari Window, individuals can examine their self-perception and identify their known strengths, weaknesses, values and beliefs, which are represented in the open or free area. Additionally, the "blind spot" reveals aspects that others may observe about us, but of which we are unaware. The hidden or façade area delves into the parts of ourselves that they keep private or selectively disclose. Lastly, the unknown area represents undiscovered aspects that are yet to be explored and understood.

However, there is a significant misconception about the level of self-awareness people believe they possess. According to surveys conducted by organisational psychologist Tasha Eurich, an overwhelming 95 per cent of individuals perceive themselves as self-aware, yet the reality is that only 10–15 per cent truly possess this quality.[30] Eurich's research delved into the complexities of self-awareness, debunking common myths and shedding light on the roadblocks and truths surrounding its nature and methods for improvement. Her findings unveil the rarity of genuine self-awareness, with only a fraction of the participants meeting the criteria for self-awareness.

Eurich's research also identified two distinct types of self-awareness. The first is internal self-awareness, which involves having a clear perception of our own values, passions, aspirations,

---

30 Tasha Eurich (2017), I*nsight: The Surprising Truth About How Others See Us, How We See Ourselves, and Why the Answers Matter More Than We Think*, Macmillan.

compatibility with our environment, reactions (including thoughts, feelings, behaviours, strengths, and weaknesses) and influence on others. Internal self-awareness correlates with higher levels of job and relationship satisfaction, personal and social control, and overall happiness. A lack of self-awareness is associated with anxiety, stress and depression.

The second type is external self-awareness, which encompasses an understanding of how others perceive us in relation to the aforementioned factors, which also aligns to the Johari Window concepts. Eurich's research revealed that individuals who possess insight into how others perceive them demonstrate greater proficiency in displaying empathy and considering others' perspectives.

Being self-aware is a vital aspect of understanding our own patterns of behaviour, motives and emotional effect on others. It enables us to identify and name our emotions, recognise triggers and comprehend why they arise. Self-awareness empowers us to acknowledge our strengths, limitations and unique abilities, tapping into our creative side to express our true selves. It involves both objective evaluation and logical analysis of who we are as individuals. By embracing our strengths, we allow our creative expression to shine and nurture our talents with passion. Simultaneously, recognising our weaknesses fosters compassion and self-acceptance, enabling us to embrace our imperfections as part of our holistic being. Through self-awareness, we embark on a journey of personal growth, driven by empathy and an understanding of our multifaceted nature.

The role of self-awareness in authenticity

Developing self-awareness is a transformative journey towards authenticity. It enables you to understand and embrace your true self by recognising your values, beliefs, strengths and weaknesses. This understanding empowers you to align your actions with your authentic self and live a purposeful and fulfilling life. As Prof Brené Brown beautifully expressed it, "Authenticity is the daily practice of letting go of who we think we're supposed to be and embracing who we are".[31] Self-awareness is the key to this practice; it helps us to navigate the following aspects of authenticity:

Recognising your values and beliefs: Self-awareness enables you to identify and clarify your core values and beliefs. It provides the foundation for making choices that align with your authentic self, rather than conforming to external expectations or societal pressures. By understanding what truly matters to you, you can live in alignment with your values and be true to yourself.

Understanding your emotions and behaviours: Self-awareness involves a deep understanding of your emotions, thoughts and behavioural patterns. It allows you to identify your emotional triggers, motivations and reactions, providing insight into why you respond to certain situations the way you do. With this awareness, you can make conscious choices and respond authentically, rather than being driven by unconscious patterns or external influences.

Embracing your strengths and weaknesses: Self-awareness encourages you to embrace both your strengths and weaknesses. It involves recognising your unique qualities, talents and skills,

---

31 Brené Brown (2010) *The Gifts of Imperfection,* Hazelden Publishing.

and acknowledging areas for growth and improvement. By embracing your authentic strengths and working on areas that need development, you can nurture your true self and contribute to the world with authenticity and purpose.

Honouring values in relationships: Self-awareness empowers you to navigate relationships authentically. By understanding your needs, boundaries and desires, you can effectively communicate them to others, establish healthy connections and surround yourself with people who respect and support your authentic self. It allows you to cultivate relationships that align with your values and promote mutual growth and understanding.

Making intentional choices: Self-awareness empowers you to make intentional choices that reflect your values, beliefs and aspirations. By understanding your authentic desires and motivations, you can navigate life with purpose and integrity. It enables you to stay true to yourself and make decisions that align with your true nature, rather than being swayed by external pressures or societal expectations.

Cultivating self-compassion and acceptance: Self-awareness involves embracing self-compassion and acceptance. It allows you to acknowledge and accept all aspects of yourself, including your imperfections and vulnerabilities. By cultivating self-compassion and self-acceptance, you can show up authentically, free from the fear of judgement or the need to conform. It enables you to love and appreciate yourself, fostering a deep sense of authenticity and wellbeing.

Developing self-awareness through self-reflection

There are many resources available to help you develop self-awareness, rumination and insight. Among these are open-source tools that anyone can access online and that have substantial research evidence supporting them. I use some of these assessment tools to help my clients better understand their motivations and drivers. Personality assessment tools such as the Myers-Briggs Type Indicator (MBTI),[32] DISC profiling[33] and Sparketype[34] are designed to enhance self-awareness and contribute to personal and professional success. These tools provide valuable insights into individual traits, preferences and behaviours. They are free and can be accessed by anyone.

While it may not come easily to everyone, developing self-awareness is an essential component of personal growth and wellbeing. Society often encourages us to prioritise logic and dismiss our emotions, leading us to detach from our true selves. However, true self-awareness requires us to courageously confront our emotions, acknowledge them and accept them as integral parts of our identity.

Cultivating self-awareness is a transformative journey that demands commitment and introspection. It requires us to delve

---

32 For example, see NERIS Analytics Limited (2011–2023), Free Personality Test (website). Accessed 11 September 20223, https://www.16personalities.com/free-personality-test

33 123test (2023), DISC Personality Test (website). Accessed 11 September 2023, https://www.123test.com/disc-personality-test/

34 Spark Endeavors Ltd (2022), Sparktype (website). Accessed 11 September 2023, https://sparketype.com/assessment/

into the depths of our thoughts, emotions and behaviours with a compassionate and non-judgemental mindset. As we embark on this path, it is essential to consider the way we frame questions to understand our motives and drivers, ensuring a kind and self-appreciating approach.

Instead of fixating on "why" questions, which can often lead to self-blame and rumination, a more constructive and empowering mindset can be fostered by asking "what" and "how" questions. These questions redirect our focus towards seeking solutions and taking proactive action. By exploring possibilities, strategies and practical steps to overcome challenges, we empower ourselves to make positive changes, reclaim agency over our lives and cultivate a sense of control.

Engaging in self-reflection and growth is another vital aspect of self-awareness. "What" and "how" questions facilitate this process by inviting us to examine our behaviours, choices and perspectives without judgement. By seeking understanding in a compassionate and non-judgemental manner, we create a nurturing space for self-compassion and self-acceptance. This space enables us to make positive changes based on our insights, and fosters personal growth and continuous learning.

Shifting our focus to "what" and "how" questions also nurture a positive mindset. Unlike "why" questions, which may invite self-criticism and reinforce limiting beliefs, "what" and "how" questions direct our attention towards our strengths, resources and possibilities. They help us identify our abilities, skills and potential for growth. By actively seeking solutions and exploring ways to improve, we reinforce a belief in our capacity to overcome obstacles. This process bolsters our self-esteem, self-efficacy and confidence, enabling us to navigate life with resilience and optimism. Some questions that can help facilitate in developing self-awareness include:

***What** are my core values and beliefs?* Understanding your values and beliefs provides a foundation for aligning your actions with your true self. For example, you may value honesty and integrity, and reflecting on how well your actions align with these values can enhance your self-awareness.

***What** motivates me?* Identifying your sources of motivation helps you gain insight into your passions, desires and aspirations. For instance, you may find that you are driven by a sense of purpose in helping others, which can shape your choices and actions.

***What** are my strengths in this area?* To identify your strengths in a particular area, reflect on activities or tasks where you feel confident and perform well. For instance, if you excel at problem-solving, embrace this as a strength. Reflect on what makes you effective in that area – perhaps it's your analytical thinking, creativity or ability to collaborate. Recognising and acknowledging your strengths contributes to self-awareness by enhancing your understanding of your unique abilities and areas where you naturally thrive.

***What** are my weaknesses?* While it is essential to embrace and leverage your strengths, it is equally important to address your weaknesses. Identify areas where you would like to improve, and develop action plans to enhance those skills or seek support from others. For example, if you struggle with time management, you could enrol in a time-management workshop, explore productivity tools or seek guidance from a time-management coach.

How do I react to stress and adversity? Reflecting on your stress-response patterns provides insight into your coping mechanisms and areas where you may need additional support or strategies. For instance, you might notice that you tend to withdraw when faced with conflict, and this could prompt you to explore healthier ways of managing such situations.

What effects do my actions have on others? Developing an awareness of how your actions and words affect those around you promotes empathy and facilitates better relationships. By reflecting on the consequences of your behaviour, you can adjust and enhance your interactions with others.

What steps can I take to achieve my goal? To develop self-awareness in pursuit of your goals, consider breaking them down into smaller, actionable steps. For example, if your goal is to improve your public-speaking skills, you could take steps such as enrolling in a public-speaking course, practising in front of a supportive audience, or seeking feedback from a mentor. By identifying specific actions, you can create a roadmap towards your goal while increasing your self-awareness of what strategies work best for you.

How can I approach this situation differently next time? When reflecting on a past situation, consider how you can approach it differently in the future. For example, if you experienced conflict with a colleague, you might explore how you could improve communication or handle disagreements more effectively. By examining alternative approaches, you can develop greater self-awareness of your default behaviours and discover new ways to respond, thereby fostering personal growth and improved outcomes.

***How** can I learn from this experience and grow?* When reflecting on an experience, consider the lessons you can draw from it. What insights can you gain about yourself, your reactions or your influence on others? For example, if you encountered a setback at work, you might reflect on how it affected your motivation or approach to challenges. By examining the experience, you can cultivate self-awareness by identifying patterns, areas for improvement and opportunities for personal growth.

Seeking feedback from others to help you grow

In addition to self-reflection, you can benefit from seeking different views from trusted individuals about how you are perceived. To develop a comprehensive understanding, it is important to approach those you trust to gain an external perspective that sheds light on unknown aspects of yourself and areas for personal growth. When you seek advice, it is essential to approach it with an open mind and a willingness to accept it without defensiveness. However, it is crucial to be selective about whom we seek opinions from, as not all feedback is constructive. Trusting and respecting the individuals' providing feedback is essential for its value.

To begin, selecting the right people to provide feedback is crucial. Look to those who know you well and who have a solid grasp of your strengths and potential areas for improvement. Colleagues, mentors or friends who can offer constructive and supportive insights make ideal candidates. Specify the aspects of your actions or performance you want input on, and find ways to facilitating meaningful and pertinent feedback. For instance, you might request advice on your communication skills, problem-solving approach or leadership style.

Having a coach or mentor we respect and trust can be particularly advantageous in this regard. During my early career, I encountered feedback and advice from individuals who failed to grasp the nuances of my unique situation as a single parent working in a male-dominated industry. Their suggestions, which questioned my career choices or urged reliance on family and friends for support, were unsuitable for my circumstances. These assumptions, differing greatly from my reality, rendered their opinions unhelpful.

And this is one of the reasons why I set up Winter & Associates. I have designed it to provide my clients with a distinct advantage by offering a trusted coach or mentor who comprehends and respects your unique circumstances. Unlike generic advice, our guidance is personalised to your situation, guaranteeing that your career choices and aspirations align with your reality, whether you're navigating a male-dominated industry or encountering other challenges. We are here to ensure you receive the personalised support required for your success.

Creating a safe and comfortable environment is vital. Ensure that conversations occur in a confidential setting where both parties feel at ease. Express your appreciation for their input and genuinely convey your openness to learning and growth. This fosters a more candid sharing of thoughts. To encourage insightful responses, use open-ended questions that prompt detailed and thoughtful feedback. Rather than seeking simple yes or no answers, inquire about specific areas for improvement or suggestions for enhancing your skills. This approach invites comprehensive insights and promotes more profound discussions.

It is important to always adopt an active listening mindset. This involves focusing intently on understanding what is being conveyed. Approach this with sincere interest, free from judgement, and dedicate your full attention to the speaker. Maintain an open posture and avoid interrupting or becoming defensive. Engage with the information being presented with a sense of curiosity, with a genuine desire to learn and grow. Reflect on the insights provided and evaluate how they align with your self-perception and what valuable lessons you can draw from them.

Another avenue is to seek out mentors who have expertise in the areas you aim to develop. Their guidance and wisdom can offer valuable perspectives and support for your personal growth. Engaging with communities or groups of like-minded individuals creates opportunities for mutual learning, sharing of experiences and support. Immersing yourself in literature, articles and online resources focused on self-development, psychology and personal growth can expand your knowledge and equip you with practical tools. Attending workshops, seminars or conferences centred on self-awareness and personal transformation can provide valuable insights and growth opportunities.

Practising mindfulness

Many online resources offer insights into various mindfulness practices. Within this sphere, I had the privilege of encountering Dr Stan Rodski, a distinguished Australian neuroscientist, at a work event in mid-2019. Dr Rodski delivered an enlightening half-day seminar on mindfulness, imparting a range of techniques for cultivating this practice. His extensive research is encapsulated in his recent publication, *The Neuroscience of Mindfulness*, which thoroughly explores an array of mindfulness methods and scrutinises their favourable effects on the nervous system.[35] A substantial part of this work related to the mind–body connection, or MBC for short.

Relating to the mind, is setting your intention to regulate your attention. This is where you place a concentrated awareness directly towards a specific point, task or sensory experience. It involves immersing yourself deeply in a singular activity, temporarily blocking out distractions, to enhance understanding and engagement. An example of focused attention can be found in the practice of playing a musical instrument. Imagine a pianist passionately playing a complex piece. Their entire focus is on the keys beneath their fingertips, the sheet music before them and the melody flowing from their instrument. In this state, the pianist is fully absorbed, honing their concentration to create a harmonious performance. The external world fades into the background as they channel their cognitive resources into producing precise notes, intricate rhythms and nuanced dynamics. This intense concentration exemplifies focused attention and allows the

---

35 Stan Rodski (2018), *The Neuroscience of Mindfulness: The astonishing science behind how everyday hobbies help you relax*, HarperCollins.

musician to execute a flawless rendition through undivided mental engagement.

Another useful practice is open monitoring of your energy. It involves non-reactive observation of your thoughts, emotions and sensations as they arise in the present moment, without judgement or attachment. It entails maintaining a detached awareness of the continuous flow of mental and sensory experiences, allowing them to come and go naturally. Just as a bystander watches a river flowing by without intervening, open monitoring cultivates a receptive and non-interfering stance towards the fluctuations of the mind, thereby fostering greater insight into patterns of thinking and emotional responses. This practice encourages a balanced and unbiased perspective and enables you to observe your inner world with clarity and equanimity.

What I love most about Dr Rodski's work is that it has an illuminating power to cultivate compassion and amplify positive emotions. The book meticulously explores how these techniques intricately shape brain activity, underscoring their neural advantages.

Outside of Rodski's work there are more traditional methods that can be employed to enhance mindfulness. Journalling is one such example. Journalling is an exceptional mindfulness tool that bolsters self-awareness. As you put your thoughts and feelings onto paper, you gain valuable insights into your emotions and acknowledge recurring behaviour patterns. Journalling also empowers you to set objectives and monitor your progress towards achieving them.

Personally, I have experienced the transformative effects of journalling. It has enabled me to process my experiences, attain clarity and pinpoint areas for personal and professional growth. Sometimes, I go back to journals I wrote many years ago and it takes me back to where I was and what I was experiencing. Such reflection brings immense gratitude for how far I have come from. Moreover, journalling has provided an outlet to release the thoughts and concerns that once kept me awake at night. Instead of ruminating over past actions, I now channel my reflections into my journal, freeing my mind from unconstructive stress and fostering healthier coping mechanisms.

If journalling is not your "thing", perhaps you could embark on practising loving-kindness meditation. This is a contemplative practice that involves cultivating feelings of compassion, benevolence and goodwill towards oneself and others. Through focused mental repetition of loving phrases or intentions, individuals extend warm and genuine wishes for happiness, peace and wellbeing to themselves, loved ones, acquaintances and even those with whom they may experience challenges. This practice nurtures a sense of interconnectedness, softens inner barriers and fosters an open-hearted and empathetic attitude, promoting emotional healing, resilience and a deepened sense of empathy and understanding.

For me, mindfulness practices have been particularly beneficial in navigating imposter syndrome, a common experience among women who work in male-dominated fields. This syndrome creates feelings of inadequacy and not belonging, despite evidence to the contrary. By engaging in mindfulness, we become aware of these thought patterns and can build a sense of self-compassion and self-acceptance that counteracts these negative feelings.

Regardless of what mindfulness activities you choose, engaging in mindfulness practice can offer you an effective path to nurture self-awareness and cultivate authenticity. Through mindfulness you can delve deeper into your internal dialogue and comprehend how it shapes your feelings and actions. Consistently practising mindfulness can significantly enhance your self-awareness, which is a cornerstone of authenticity.

Understanding your strengths and weaknesses

Understanding your strengths and weaknesses is an important aspect of being authentic. It allows you to have a clear understanding of yourself, and how you can best strive in your work and personal life. Over my career, I have come to understand the importance of recognising my own strengths and weaknesses to be an effective leader and team member.

One way we can do this is through self-reflection. It involves taking the time to think about our experiences, actions and behaviours, and identifying what we did well and what we could improve upon. It can be helpful to write these down and review them regularly to track progress and continue self-improvement.

Personal strengths can also become evident to others through various observations. Ways that strengths are noticed by others include comments relating to consistent excellence in specific tasks, a natural aptitude for leadership and the ability to inspire stand out. You may be "called out" for effective problem-solving skills, along with remarkable communication and empathy, or the ability to catch people's attention in the right way. Additionally, a consistent display of determination and resilience could be recognised as a talent for creative thinking and innovation. A willingness to help and collaborate, coupled with strong organisational skills, is often noted. Furthermore, a positive influence on others' wellbeing and a commitment to continuous learning and growth become evident over time.

Others can communicate weaknesses in a variety of ways. Constructive feedback is often given, highlighting areas that require improvement. They might point out challenges or recurring difficulties in certain tasks, shedding light on specific weaknesses. Concerns about skills or abilities could be raised, coupled with suggestions for skill development or training. Instances where weaknesses may have affected outcomes could be shared, along with alternative approaches to addressing shortcomings. Observations of limitations in various contexts might be discussed, and instances where weaknesses could affect collaboration or performance could be noted. In some cases, they may suggest seeking additional support or resources to overcome these weaknesses. It can be difficult to hear criticism, but it is important to approach it with an open mind and a willingness to learn and improve.

In understanding our strengths, we can leverage them to be more effective in our work and personal lives. For example, if we are good at problem-solving, we can seek out opportunities to solve challenging problems in our work, or volunteer to help others with their own problems. On the other hand, recognising our weaknesses allows us to take steps to improve or find ways to work around them. For example, if we struggle with public speaking, we can seek out training or practise speaking in front of a smaller audience before presenting to a larger group.

However, it is important to remember that our strengths and weaknesses are not fixed, and can change over time. As we gain new experiences and skills, our strengths may evolve or shift, and our weaknesses may become less of a challenge. It is important to continue to reflect on and assess our strengths and weaknesses, to ensure we are staying true to our authentic selves.

It can be challenging to confront our weaknesses and vulnerabilities, but it is essential to embrace them, to fully understand ourselves and live an authentic life. By acknowledging our weaknesses, we can approach them with a growth mindset and see them as opportunities for self-improvement. By embracing our vulnerabilities, we can build deeper connections with others and create a fulfilling life.

Arianna Huffington[36], the founder of the Huffington Post, once wrote, "We need to accept that we won't always make the right decisions, that we'll screw up royally sometimes – understanding that failure is not the opposite of success, it's part of success."

By developing self-awareness, you can learn from your failures and mistakes, identify your strengths and weaknesses, and ultimately become more authentic in your personal and professional life.

---

36 Arianna Huffington (2019). Twitter Post (20 May). Accessed 27 September 2023, https://twitter.com/ariannahuff/status/1130172552352063489?lang=en

9

Building Your
Self-Confidence

Building self-confidence, believing in oneself, and embracing authenticity are essential ingredients for a fulfilling and empowered life. As Amelia Earhart, the pioneering aviator, was once quoted saying, "The most effective way to do it is to do it".[37] I think that this statement captures the essence of the journey towards self-confidence and self-belief. Just as a strong foundation supports a sturdy structure, developing a solid sense of self-confidence provides the bedrock upon which we can build a life true to our authentic selves. By cultivating self-assurance, trusting our abilities and embracing our uniqueness, we can navigate life's challenges with resilience, pursue our dreams with determination and have a positive effect on the world. Embracing authenticity allows individuals to connect with their true selves, and leads to

37 https://www.ameliaearhart.com/quotes/

greater fulfilment, contentment and harmony within themselves and the world around them.

Authenticity is closely tied to having a strong sense of self-confidence. However, achieving authenticity can prove challenging, especially when grappling with self-doubt or attempting to control every aspect of life. In such situations, people may resort to imposing their will on others or wearing a facade, which results in a disconnection from their true identity. This disconnection can lead to emotional struggles and anxiety, depression and other mental health problems.

As I look back on my early life, I can identify moments where I tried to control people and situations, seeking to find balance and normality. I believed that having control would ensure the desired outcomes. Unfortunately, this approach proved ineffective and had a detrimental effect on my relationships, particularly with my children. Interestingly, I realised that this behaviour mirrored that of my father, who had sought to control everything, including his children's lives. Growing up in such an environment shattered my self-confidence, and I subconsciously adopted the same tactics to regain a sense of control in my life.

I discovered that emulating my father's controlling ways only led to similar negative results with my own daughters. It was not until the early 2000s, when my life hit rock bottom after the failure of my second marriage, that I had a moment of awakening. I realised that true control lay in believing in myself and my capabilities. I understood that I could control only my own actions, thoughts and feelings, not those of others, nor their opinions of me. It was a crucial turning point where I acknowledged the need to unlearn toxic habits instilled in me from my upbringing. To be genuinely happy with myself and my actions, I needed to embrace my authenticity and possess genuine self-confidence.

The process of self-discovery and shedding those toxic habits was far from instant. In fact, it took more than a decade of making mistakes, exploring different avenues and truly understanding who I was and what I wanted before I could honestly say that I had embraced my authenticity and developed genuine self-confidence. The journey was arduous but immensely rewarding. I now stand empowered with the understanding that being true to myself, acknowledging my worth and trusting in my abilities are the keys to living an authentic and fulfilled life.

Gaining self-confidence empowers individuals to embrace their authentic selves effortlessly and to live a fulfilling life. Self-assurance enables them to remain true to their genuine selves, to express themselves sincerely and navigate life authentically. This self-confidence fosters a strong sense of fulfilment and alignment with personal values and beliefs, contributing to a healthier and more contented existence.

One way to understand the relationship between self-confidence and authenticity is through a fable. Imagine a young bird who wants to learn how to fly. The bird knows that it has wings, but it is afraid to use them. It lacks self-confidence and is afraid of failing. One day, the bird meets an older, wiser bird who tells it a secret: "To fly, you must first believe that you can."

The young bird takes this advice to heart and begins to practise using its wings. It starts by taking small hops, then gradually works up to longer flights. With each success, its self-confidence grows, and it becomes more and more authentic as it becomes more comfortable with its abilities.

Like the young bird, we all sometimes need a little push to get started. Developing self-confidence is a crucial first step to being authentic. When we believe in ourselves and our abilities, we are more likely to take risks and be true to ourselves.

Steps in developing self-confidence

Numerous resources, including articles, books and activities, are available to assist in enhancing your self-confidence. I have compiled a list of recommended readings from my own experiences (see page 189), but it is important to identify that the path to boosting self-confidence is deeply individual. Through my personal journey and as a mentor and coach for others, I have come to understand that a tailored approach is essential: there is no universal solution. The effectiveness of a strategy hinges on our individual strengths, weaknesses and inclinations, be it a preference for logic or emotion. The crucial point is to experiment and to integrate successful methods into our daily routines and sustaining them over time.

I recall receiving valuable advice about changing certain behaviours: that the changes we make should be sustainable over the long term. While it may feel challenging or awkward initially, with persistence and consistency these changes can lead to a natural growth in self-confidence over time. Drawing inspiration from James Clear's book, *Atomic Habits*,[38] which highlights the

---

38 James Clear (2018), *Atomic Habits*, Penguin Random House.

power of small, incremental changes, I have seen the positive effect of focusing on daily habits. Clear's four-step framework for building effective habits is especially relevant:

Make habits obvious: Identify cues or triggers that prompt your desired behaviours, and create an environment that encourages these habits.

Make habits attractive: Linking your habits to positive emotions and rewards makes them more appealing and likely to be repeated.

Make habits easy: Break down habits into manageable, achievable tasks to increase consistency and success.

Make habits satisfying: Ensure that your habits offer intrinsic or extrinsic rewards; this fosters motivation and satisfaction in your progress.

Implementing the concept of "habit stacking" – building new habits upon existing routines – can be transformative, and tracking progress is essential for maintaining our motivation.

Furthermore, shaping our self-image and identity plays a significant role in achieving lasting behaviour change and ultimately can lead to enhanced self-confidence. By incorporating these strategies into your daily life and staying committed to personal growth, you can steadily build your self-confidence and enjoy the lasting improvements it brings.

One effective approach involves utilising positive self-talk. If this seems like a significant leap initially, begin by eliminating negative words from your thoughts and statements. Consider the frequency with which you might have heard someone describe themselves as "just a..." – a seemingly insignificant phrase that carries substantial implications. Imagine the potential if you fully embraced the power of your words. Distinguish yourself as a daughter, mother, engineer, scientist and much more. The word "just", when positioned before a statement, has the tendency to undercut or devalue its significance. Yet, women do it far more frequently than we realise. "Just" implies that we are incomplete or lacking in some way, and this can lead to unnecessary comparisons with others or with societal ideals. This type of self-talk can be particularly damaging to our self-confidence, often perpetuating negative beliefs about our own abilities.

Personally, I have experienced the benefits of this approach, becoming more mindful of how I speak to myself. I make it a point to gently remind others to adopt the same practice when I hear them unintentionally using self-deprecating language. It is essential to recognise that words hold great significance.

Rather than being our own critics, we should be our own cheerleaders. Instead of telling ourselves what we cannot do, we should use positive language to encourage a shift in our thinking, by focusing on our strengths and achievements. For instance, instead of saying "I am no good at public speaking", we can reframe it as "I am continuously improving my public speaking skills and becoming more confident when I present in public". Or more broadly, instead of thinking, "I'm not good enough," reframe it to, "I am capable and have overcome challenges. I am deserving of success". By making this shift in language, we send a powerful and uplifting message to ourselves, thereby reinforcing positive behaviours.

PERSONAL REFLECTION
A self-confidence hack

One of the most effective methods I have encountered for building self-confidence is setting achievable goals. I began implementing this approach during my time at university, when I was 34 years old. At that time, I was burdened with self-doubt, haunted by discouraging words from a female Commander who believed I would never make it through the first semester of university, because I had not finished high school and was a single parent.

To overcome these doubts, I decided to set a specific and attainable goal for that semester. Rather than aiming to complete the entire degree or even the first year, which seemed overwhelming, I focused on passing four subjects with a distinction average. I further broke down my target by aiming to achieve 60–80 per cent in each assessment, to maintain an average for the semester above 70 per cent.

This approach gave me some leeway in case I encountered challenges and also embraced the satisfaction of accomplishing smaller milestones when I enjoyed the topics I was studying. By setting realistic and manageable goals, I could build my confidence gradually and steadily progress towards success in my academic pursuits.

Arianna Huffington underscored the significance of cultivating a resilient self in her book *Thrive*, noting its role in diminishing susceptibility to external opinions and assessments.[39] She highlighted that possessing a sturdy sense of self lessens our susceptibility to the influence of others' judgements. This fortification shields us from being easily swayed by external situations or the fluctuations of life; it fosters a rooted and

---

39 Arianna Huffington (2014), *Thrive*, Penguin Random House.

unwavering identity that enhances our resilience. However, it all begins with self-belief: the conviction that we have the capability to achieve anything we set our minds to. This self-assurance empowers us to follow through with our intentions and pursue our goals with determination and unwavering commitment.

Setting goals and celebrating small victories

When we establish goals for ourselves, we set a clear sense of direction and purpose, which serves as a powerful motivator. It is crucial to set goals that strike a balance between being challenging and realistic. A goal that is too easy may lack a sense of fulfilment once achieved, while an excessively difficult goal can demotivate us if progress seems unattainable. The key is to set objectives that challenge us and yet remain achievable.

Setting goals to build self-confidence is akin to ascending a ladder. The closer the rungs of the ladder are, the easier the climb. Just as in the journey of self-improvement, setting manageable objectives and devising a methodical strategy form the rungs of our ladder, allowing us to climb with steady assurance. Navigating this ascent requires us to maintain an emotional rapport with ourselves, celebrating each accomplishment, and fostering self-kindness throughout our expedition. A practical approach involves plotting rewards along this ladder of progress, ensuring that our path is peppered with gratifying milestones that reinforce our upward stride.

Much like climbing a ladder, my academic journey was marked with deliberate steps. Each assessment became a rung that I focused on intently, meticulously mapping out my route to success. Just as the rungs of a ladder are spaced closely for an easier climb, I ensured that my goals were achievable and progressive. To further amplify my sense of achievement, I positioned small yet meaningful rewards at the end of each milestone. For instance, at the close of the semester, if I had achieved a good grade, I celebrated with a well-deserved night out with friends. The moments of choosing study over socialising became more rewarding and etched in memory when I eventually embraced those outings. Much like planning stops along a journey, I infused my path with motivation by orchestrating special events, such as witnessing my favourite bands perform or seizing the opportunity to attend exclusive shows, all contributing to a well-rounded and gratifying climb.

This tradition of celebrating achievements continues in my life, even now with my husband. We plan nights out to attend events or to engage in unique activities, which gives a sense of excitement and motivation. This practice not only focuses me on my small yet achievable goals but also reminds me to cherish every moment and relish the joy of accomplishment.

When we achieve something, regardless of its scale, it is vital to pause and acknowledge our accomplishments. This recognition encourages a sense of achievement and propels us towards bigger goals. Furthermore, celebrating our successes enables us to appreciate our worth and the unique contributions we bring.

Cultivating a supportive network

As identified in Chapter 8, a way to increase self-confidence is to seek information and support from those we look up to. Professor Ken Blanchard, renowned speaker and consultant in leadership and management once wrote that, *"Feedback is the breakfast of champions".*[40] This insightful statement underscores the significance of actively seeking (useful) advice and using it as a catalyst for growth and improvement. As a female engineer, I have personally experienced the tremendous value of seeking feedback from colleagues and supervisors whom I admired and respected. It has been instrumental in building my self-confidence and refining my skills.

While conventional wisdom often suggests that feedback should primarily come from senior or older individuals, I challenge this notion. I regularly seek views from both my supervisors and my juniors, understanding that valuable insights can be gleaned from people with diverse experiences and perspectives. I firmly believe that learning is not limited by age or seniority; I can gain just as much from a junior, less experienced person as I can from a more seasoned individual.

Further to this, surrounding ourselves with supportive and positive people who uplift and encourage us is vital. It is equally crucial to limit exposure to individuals who undermine our self-belief or bring negativity into our lives. By cultivating a nurturing environment, we create space for self-confidence to flourish and

---

40 Feedback is the Breakfast of Champions, *Ken Blanchard Books,* 17 August 2009. Accessed 26 September 2023, https://www.kenblanchardbooks.com/feedback-is-the-breakfast-of-champions/

to embrace our true potential. As human beings, we are greatly influenced by the people around us, and their attitudes and beliefs can have a powerful effect on our self-perception. By intentionally seeking out people who believe in and support us, we can boost our self-confidence and feel secure in our own abilities and potential.

This can be particularly important in male-dominated industries, where women may feel isolated or unsupported. Seek out mentors and allies who can offer advice, guidance and support as you navigate your career path. You can also look for networking groups or professional associations that are specifically designed to support women in your field. By connecting with others who share your experiences and challenges, you can build a sense of community and support that can help to boost your confidence and sense of belonging. For professional women, this may mean seeking out mentors, or networking with other successful women in your field. By connecting with other women who have similar experiences and challenges, you can gain valuable insights and advice, as well as emotional support and encouragement. Consider joining professional organisations and attending conferences or workshops where you can meet and learn from other women in your industry.

It is important to remember that building self-confidence is not a one-time event or achievement, but rather a continuous process of growth and development. There will be setbacks and challenges along the way, but with determination and perseverance, anyone can become more self-assured and confident in themselves and their abilities.

One example of a successful professional woman who has used these strategies to build her self-confidence is Indra Nooyi, the former CEO of PepsiCo. Nooyi has spoken publicly about the challenges she faced as a woman and a person of colour in the corporate world, and the importance of surrounding oneself with supportive people.

In a 2018 interview with CNBC, Nooyi stated, "When you're in a company and you're trying to break the glass ceiling, it's not easy... But I think the key is to find people who support you, who believe in you, and who will champion you... It's really important to surround yourself with those kinds of people." [41]

Nooyi also emphasised the importance of setting achievable goals and celebrating small victories, stating, "You have to have small wins along the way... You can't just say, 'I'm going to become CEO tomorrow.' You have to say, 'What are the small things I need to do along the way?' And every time you achieve one of those small things, you need to celebrate it."

The role of self-compassion in building self-confidence

Self-compassion is an essential component of building self-confidence and is particularly important for women who often face unique challenges and barriers in professional settings. Self-compassion involves treating oneself with kindness,

41 CNBC TV8 (2023), Indra Nooyi Talks About Her Journey & More (video recording, 12 June). Accessed 11 September 2023, https://www.youtube.com/watch?v=_LKbBq1RD40

understanding, and empathy, rather than being overly critical or judgemental. It means recognising and accepting that we are not perfect and that making mistakes is a normal part of the learning process.

In a professional setting, self-compassion can help women develop the confidence to take risks and try new things, without fear of failure or the negative opinions of others. It can also help women navigate the inevitable setbacks and challenges that arise in any career.

CASE STUDY
Cultivating self-compassion

Sarah, a young engineer, recently started a new job at a large construction company. She was excited about the opportunity but soon found that she was the only woman in her department, which made her feel self-conscious and insecure.

Sarah's lack of self-confidence was affecting her ability to perform her job effectively. She was afraid to speak up in meetings, and her work was suffering as a result. She also found herself constantly comparing herself to her male colleagues, feeling inadequate and questioning her abilities.

Through working with me as her coach, Sarah was able to recognise the importance of self-compassion in building self-confidence. She began to practise self-compassion by treating herself with kindness and understanding, rather than being overly critical of her mistakes or shortcomings. She learned to realise that her lack of self-confidence was not a reflection of her abilities or worth as a person, but rather the result of societal expectations and the pressures of working in a male-dominated industry. She began to challenge these expectations and to embrace her unique perspective and skills.

Through coaching I was able to encourage Sarah to set achievable goals for herself. Each fortnight we would get together as discuss her achievements and setbacks. I was able to assist her in recognising and celebrating the small victories, which helped to build her confidence over time. She learned to focus on her strengths and to use them to her advantage, rather than trying to conform to the expectations of others.

Through the practice of self-compassion, Sarah was able to overcome her imposter syndrome and to build the confidence she needed to succeed in her career. She learned that self-compassion is not a weakness but rather a strength, and that by treating herself with kindness and understanding, she could be a more effective and fulfilled professional.

In her own words: "When I started at that construction company, I felt like I had something to prove. I worked long hours and tried to be perfect in everything I did. But the more I tried to be perfect, the more I felt like I was failing. I was constantly comparing myself to my male colleagues, who seemed to be more confident and successful than I was. I felt like an imposter, like I didn't belong there."

During one of our coaching sessions, Sarah shared with me that she felt like she was not good enough to be in her position. She had been passed over for a promotion and felt like a failure. Through our conversation, Sarah realised that she was being too hard on herself and that her self-talk was fuelling her imposter syndrome.

After she struggled with this for several months, I encouraged Sarah to seek ways she could overcome these self-confidence destroying habits. She enrolled in a mindfulness-based stress reduction (MBSR) program. Through guided meditation and self-reflection, Sarah learned to observe her thoughts and emotions without judgement.

She also began to admit the negative self-talk that was holding her back.

Together, we worked on her cultivating self-compassion, which involves treating herself with kindness, understanding and forgiveness. Sarah began to practise self-compassion by speaking to herself as she would to a friend. She reminded herself that making mistakes was a natural part of the learning process and that her worth was not tied to her job title or her achievements.

As Sarah practised self-compassion, she began to feel more confident in her abilities. She started taking on more challenging projects and speaking up in meetings. She realised that she did not need to be perfect to be successful and that self-compassion was a powerful tool for building self-confidence. Eventually, Sarah was offered a promotion and was excited to take on the new role. She appreciated that her success was not just due to her hard work, but also to her willingness to be vulnerable and to practise self-compassion.

Adopting a mindset of self-compassion can be challenging, especially in the face of societal pressures and the demands of a fast-paced professional environment. However, with practice, it is possible to build self-compassion and to use it as a powerful tool for building self-confidence and resilience.

In the words of Kristin Neff, a leading researcher on self-compassion, "Self-compassion is simply giving the same kindness to ourselves that we would give to others".[42] By treating ourselves with the same kindness and empathy we would show to a friend or

---

42 Kristin Neff (2011), *Self Compassion: Stop beating yourself up and leave insecurity behind*, Yellow Kite, Hachette.

loved one, we can build the self-confidence and resilience needed to succeed in any professional setting.

A final word regarding self-compassion. It is a powerful tool for building self-confidence and overcoming imposter syndrome. By treating ourselves with kindness and understanding, we can let go of the need to be perfect and embrace our true selves. As women in male-dominated fields, it can be easy to fall into the trap of comparing ourselves to others and feeling like we do not belong. But with self-compassion, we can admit that we are all human and deserving of love and respect, including from ourselves.

10

Trusting Your Intuition

"The only limit to your impact is your
imagination and commitment."

TONY ROBBINS [43]

Within each of us lies a powerful compass that can guide us on our journey through life. As supermodel Gisele Bundchen once wisely stated, "The more you trust your intuition, the more empowered you become, the stronger you become, and the happier you become".[44] Her insight beautifully captures the essence of honouring our inner voice and the significance of trusting our intuition. Just as a compass points us in the right direction, our intuition serves as an unwavering guide, leading us towards choices and paths that align with our true selves. By

---

43 Tony Robbins (2017), Twitter post (21 February). Accessed 11 September 2023, https://twitter.com/TonyRobbins/status/833720634764976129

44 Gisele Bundchen Quotes. (n.d.). BrainyQuote.com. Accessed 12 August 2023 https://www.brainyquote.com/quotes/gisele_bundchen_412233

embracing and following this inner compass, we unlock a strong sense of empowerment, strength, and happiness, allowing us to navigate life's challenges with authenticity and clarity.

The connection between self-trust and intuition is deeply intertwined. Your self-trust serves as the bedrock for having confidence in your decisions and skills, while your intuition offers you an instinctual grasp of various situations. As your self-trust strengthens, you will find yourself more likely to embrace and follow your intuitive hunches, distinguishing them as trustworthy guides. This synergy facilitates decision-making that is better aligned and more knowledgeable, reflecting your genuine self.

Intuition becomes a potent ally, guiding you towards your genuine self. Within you resides a subtle yet mighty force, offering insights and direction for your journey. It is often called the "inner voice", and tuning into your intuition leads to wiser choices, enriched relationships and a more fulfilling existence. Embracing this inner compass involves evaluating perspectives, weighing logic and making informed choices. Validation comes through acknowledging your feelings, embracing synchronicities and decoding the subtle messages that emanate from your intuitive core.

Research shows that intuition is not just a mystical concept, but a real and important aspect of decision-making. A study conducted by the University of Leeds found that people who relied on their intuition made more accurate decisions than those who relied solely on logic.[45] Trusting your intuition can be especially important for women in male-dominated fields, where the pressure to conform to societal expectations can be strong. Several articles and studies published in the *Harvard Business Review*[46] found that listening to your inner voice makes you a better manager, and that women in leadership positions who trusted their intuition were more successful than those who did not.

At its essence, intuition brings immediate understanding, bypassing conscious reasoning. It draws from your experiences, beliefs and emotions, serving as a unique well of wisdom. When you are attuned to your intuition, decisions align with your values and this fosters trust in yourself and amplifies your confidence. In a world valuing rationality, trusting our intuition might pose a challenge, yet it is integral to an authentic life. If you are an engineer or professional in other STEM disciplines, cultivating this trust involves drawing insights from your experiences, assembling data and uncovering patterns to corroborate your instincts. Nurturing your emotional side through mindfulness, creative efforts like meditation or art, and attuning to your soul's whispers makes heeding your intuition a more natural process.

---

45 Science Daily (2008), Go With Your Gut – Intuition Is More Than Just A Hunch, Says New Research (webpage). Accessed 11 September 2023, https://www.sciencedaily.com/releases/2008/03/080305144210.htm

46 Jack Zenger and Joseph Folkman (2019), Research: Women score higher than men in most leadership skills, *Harvard Business Review*, 18 June. Accessed 11 September 2023, https://hbr.org/2019/06/research-women-score-higher-than-men-in-most-leadership-skills; Cindy Gallop and Tomas Chamorro-Premuzic (2021), 7 pieces of bad career advice women should ignore, *Harvard Business Review*, 15 April. Accessed 11 September 2023, https://hbr.org/2021/04/7-pieces-of-bad-career-advice-women-should-ignore; Vineet Nayar (2015), Listening to your inner voices makes you a better manager, *Harvard Business Review*, 13 May. Accessed 11 September 2023, https://hbr.org/2013/05/listening-to-your-inner-voice

CASE STUDY
Trusting your intuition

For example, consider the story of Zara, a young engineer who was offered a job at a prestigious company. The job was highly competitive and came with a significant salary increase, but something about the opportunity did not sit right with her. Although she could not quite put her finger on it, she had a nagging feeling that this job was not the right fit for her. Zara's friends and family urged her to take the job, telling her that it was too good an opportunity to pass up. However, despite the pressure she was under, Zara decided to trust her intuition and turned down the job offer.

A few months later, Zara found a job with a smaller company that was a much better fit for her personality and career goals. Although the salary was not as high as the first job offer, she felt much more fulfilled and happier in her new role. Looking back, Zara realised that her intuition had been guiding her towards the right decision all along. Zara's story is a great example of how trusting our intuition can lead to positive outcomes. When we listen to our inner voice, we are more likely to make decisions that align with our authentic selves, even if they go against the expectations of others.

Strategies for trusting your intuition

Tap into your body's wisdom. To fortify your trust in intuition and respect your inner voice, you should practise feeling and appreciating the signals it imparts. Allocate moments for self-reflection on your experiences and emotions, nurturing the assurance that emanates from within. As you uncover logical underpinnings that affirm the credibility of your intuitive guidance, relying on your inner voice will come more naturally and will be empowering.

As part of Dr Rodski's MBC mindfulness practices he encourages us to listen closely to our physical sensations and emotions in various situations and decision-making moments. He asserts that the body holds valuable insights about what aligns with our instincts. For instance, if you encounter a decision that seems logical but conflicts with your intuition, take a moment to check in with yourself. Observe if you feel a sense of expansion or contraction in your body, indicating whether it aligns with your intuition.

Be fully present in conversations with others. To enhance this ability, practise active listening by focusing on their words, tone, body language and energy. Trust your intuitive sense to grasp underlying messages beyond explicit expressions. During meetings or discussions, pay attention to any intuitive nudges or insights that arise. Being fully present and attentive while trusting your intuition allows you to understand unspoken messages conveyed through non-verbal cues. This promotes empathy and fosters deeper connections with others, enhancing trust and communication. By trusting your intuition during interactions, you can sense emotions and needs beyond what is explicitly expressed, and this empowers you to respond and support others effectively.

As a coach and mentor, I place great importance on observing not only what is being said but also what is left unsaid, along with body language incongruences. Albert Mehrabian's research highlights that communication is 55 per cent non-verbal, 38 per cent vocal and 7 per cent words only.[47] Trusting my gut instincts plays a key role in helping me discern whether the spoken words align with the individual's truth.

As a coach, spotting inconsistencies is crucial in my work to guide clients towards identifying solutions. Encouraging them to trust their own instincts and intuition empowers them to make informed decisions. This comprehensive approach enhances relationships, creates a more meaningful social environment and facilitates better understanding and communication with others.

Reflect on past experiences. Look back on instances where you trusted your intuition and it led you towards positive outcomes. Recall the feelings you had during those moments and the results that followed. Use these past experiences as evidence to strengthen your trust in your intuition. For instance, think about a time when you followed a strong intuitive feeling and it turned out to be beneficial. Reflect on how that experience affirmed the importance of trusting your intuition.

For me, a significant positive reflection on trusting my intuition occurred when I met my current husband. Despite my logical brain analysing practical aspects like distance, financial and emotional situations, I chose to follow my gut instinct for a change. This decision proved to be the best one I have ever made. Not only is my husband a supportive and nurturing partner, but I also learned that my previous conditioning to be overly logical did not always serve me well. Trusting my intuition on that occasion

---

47 Albert Mehrabian and M. Wiener (1967). Decoding of inconsistent communications, *Journal of Personality and Social Psychology, 6*(1), 109–114.

brought immense joy and fulfilment into my life, teaching me the value of listening to my inner voice.

Embrace the unknown and be open to uncertainty. Intuition often becomes more apparent when we let go of the need for complete control and certainty. When facing new opportunities or changes, recognise that your intuition may guide you in unexpected directions. Trust that the unknown holds the potential for growth and self-discovery. You can start by making small decisions based on your intuition and observing the outcomes. As you experience positive results, your trust in your intuitive guidance will strengthen.

For example, in a work setting, you might have a gut feeling that a particular project proposal is not aligned with your team's capabilities or long-term goals. However, due to pressure from higher-ups or fear of disappointing others, you decide to go along with it. As the project progresses, you may notice signs of strain within the team, missed deadlines and a lack of enthusiasm. These outcomes could be an indication that you went against your intuition, which initially identified the project's potential challenges. Reflecting on this experience can reinforce the importance of trusting your instincts in professional settings, as it can lead to more positive and harmonious outcomes.

Trusting your intuition is a powerful tool that can guide you towards authenticity and fulfilment in life. Just as a compass points us in the right direction, our intuition serves as a steadfast guide, leading us towards choices and paths that align with our true selves. By embracing the unknown and being open to uncertainty, we create space for our intuition to speak loudest, provide valuable insights and guide us towards growth and self-discovery. In a world that often prioritises rational thinking, learning to listen to our inner voice is essential for leading an authentic life. By cultivating trust in our intuition, we gain confidence in ourselves and our abilities, which empowers us to navigate life's challenges with clarity and purpose.

Understanding the difference between intuition and fear-based thinking

Trusting your intuition empowers you to navigate life's paths, but it is vital to discern intuition from fear-driven thoughts. Your intuition often propels you towards risk-taking and stepping beyond familiar boundaries, prompting decisions that might challenge societal norms or established wisdom. These choices, however, will lead you towards a life that resonates with your genuine aspirations and true identity. On the other hand, fear-based thinking emerges from insecurities, uncertainties and negative beliefs, obscuring your judgement and steering you away from your authentic self. It originates from your survival instinct and is often influenced by past encounters or conditioning. While designed to ensure your safety, it can also hinder you from embracing risks and pursuing your aspirations.

In retrospect, as I reflect upon my life's journey, I have come to fully acknowledge that a significant portion of my military service was driven by fear: of failure, inadequacy and self-doubt. The weight of this recognition is evident in the anxiety and tension that enveloped me during that time. These deeply ingrained beliefs served as constricting barriers, impeding my ability to fully embrace my own views. Since my departure from the military, I have embarked on a journey of growth where I have honed the skill of heeding my intuition and gut instincts. I have adopted a questioning approach, consistently asking myself: How do I feel? Do I sense excitement, or do I harbour apprehension? These markers have become my guideposts, helping me discern whether my decisions are rooted in fear or intuition.

Trusting your intuition takes courage and practice. It requires you to tune out external "noise" and distractions and to turn inward to listen to your inner voice. It may mean making decisions that are not popular, or going against the grain, but ultimately, it will lead to a more fulfilling and authentic life. Some strategies I have used to cultivate my intuition and trust in myself include:

Practising active listening: This has been instrumental for me in developing a heightened intuition. By attentively and empathetically listening to others, I have learned to pick up on subtle nuances and underlying emotions, unveiling their genuine intentions and feelings.

Engaging in creative expression: Whether through art, music or writing, this has been a powerful avenue for tapping into my intuition. Creative outlets allow me to freely express myself without judgement, unlocking parts of my subconscious that might otherwise remain concealed and revealing unique insights and ideas.

Spending quality time in nature: This practice has significantly deepened my connection with my inner voice and bolstered my intuition. Scientific research has underscored the stress-reducing effects of being in nature, fostering a sense of calm and relaxation that, in turn, amplifies my intuitive capacity.

Practising gratitude: Directing my focus towards the aspects of my life that I am grateful for has cultivated a positive mindset and heightened self-awareness, ultimately strengthening my ability to spot and wholeheartedly rely on my intuition. This has proven pivotal in nurturing self-trust and amplifying my intuitive prowess.

Engaging in regular physical activity: My anxiety is now gone and my stress is very much under control. Through exercise, I have cultivated a greater connection with my body, and self-awareness that in turn enhances my receptivity to intuitive insights.

While these strategies might not resonate with everyone, they can serve as valuable instruments for nurturing trust and intuition in your daily existence. Consistently engaging in these techniques can help you to foster a heightened self-awareness and forge a deeper bond with your inner wisdom, ultimately guiding you towards a life that is enriched, genuine and authentic.

In closing, trusting your intuition is a powerful way to navigate life authentically and to lead a fulfilling existence. It involves embracing your inner voice, spotting the distinction between intuition and fear-based thinking, and actively listening to your gut feelings and insights. By learning from past experiences and reflecting on positive outcomes resulting from following your intuition, you can strengthen your trust in this inner wisdom. Making small decisions based on intuition and observing the positive results further reinforces this trust. Additionally, mindfulness practices and being fully present in conversations with others allow you to understand unspoken messages conveyed through tone, body language and energy, promoting empathy and deeper connections. Trusting your intuition empowers you to make choices that align with your true self and leads to more authentic and successful paths in life. By embracing uncertainty and being open to the unknown, you create space for your intuition to guide you towards growth and self-discovery. Ultimately, cultivating trust in your intuition enables you to live an authentic, fulfilling life in which you make decisions that are aligned with your values and aspirations.

11

How to Align Your Actions with Your Authentic Self

Living authentically is the art of harmonising our actions with the truest essence of who we are and navigating through life's symphony with grace and conviction.

As former United States First Lady Michelle Obama said, "I have learned that as long as I hold fast to my beliefs and values – and follow my own moral compass – then the only expectations I need to live up to are my own".[48] I think this statement beautifully captures the essence of aligning our actions with our authentic

---

48 Tuskegee Virtual Tv (2015), Michelle Obama Speaks at Tuskegee University (video recording, 09 May). Accessed 26 September 2023, https://www.youtube.com/watch?v=qhUKwl5NFgE

selves. It is akin to being a dancer who confidently moves to their own rhythm in a world filled with orchestras.

Living authentically means being true to yourself and aligning your actions with your core values, beliefs and identity. This may sound simple, but it requires a deep understanding of oneself and the courage to make decisions that align with our authentic self. To align your actions with your authentic self, it's beneficial to engage in self-assessment and identify areas of incongruence between your beliefs and behaviours. As a coach, I have witnessed firsthand the transformative power of living authentically, and I strongly believe that it is the key to living a fulfilling and meaningful life.

Living authentically involves embracing vulnerability, being open to personal growth and transformation, and trusting the process of self-discovery to guide your actions. It requires a willingness to be honest with yourself about what truly matters to you. It means acknowledging your values, beliefs, strengths and weaknesses, and using them as a guide for your actions. It also means being aware of the external pressures and societal expectations that may be influencing your decisions, and intentionally choosing to stay true to yourself.

As mentioned to earlier, encountering Dr Wayne Dyer's work played a significant role in my journey of self-discovery. I had the privilege of meeting him personally and listening to him speak multiple times. Dr Dyer's influence in the field of personal development and spiritual growth has been immense. One of his powerful statements, "Doing what you love is the cornerstone of having abundance in your life",[49] holds great meaning for me. It underscores the importance of aligning our actions with our authentic selves. When we follow our passions and engage in work and activities we love, we become enthusiastic, motivated, and fulfilled in both our personal and professional lives. It is in this alignment with our true selves that we find purpose and abundance.

Conversely, when we stray from our authentic path, we may experience feelings of depletion, dissatisfaction and a sense of disconnection from our purpose. Dr Dyer's teachings have reinforced the significance of embracing our true selves and living in harmony with our inner values and passions. By doing so, we can unlock the potential for abundance and fulfilment in our lives, as we navigate our journey with purpose and authenticity.

Identifying core values is an introspective process that involves self-reflection and exploration. Until this point, this book has offered insights as to what your journey to aligning with your authentic self may look like. Start by considering what truly matters to you in life and what principles you hold dear. Reflect on moments when you felt most fulfilled, happy and aligned with your authentic self.

Ask yourself what qualities and virtues you admire in others and aspire to embody. Consider the aspects of life that bring you a sense of purpose and meaning. Journalling, meditation and discussions with trusted friends or mentors can also aid in this self-discovery journey. Pay attention to moments when you feel

---

49 Wayne W. Dyer Quotes (n.d.). BrainyQuote.com. Accessed 12 August 2023.
   https://www.brainyquote.com/quotes/wayne_dyer_173497

a strong emotional reaction, positive or negative, as they often point to underlying values. With time and reflection, you will uncover the core values that form a solid foundation upon which you can align your actions and live authentically.

MY PERSONAL JOURNEY
The Winter promise

When I was formulating the foundation of my coaching business and defining my values, I embarked on a reflective process to discover what truly resonated with me. Interestingly, the WINTER acronym emerged as a powerful symbol. First, it bears the name of my beloved dog, who symbolises joy and happiness, qualities I wish to inspire in my clients' lives. Second, it is an acronym for Women In Non-Traditional Employment Roles, which holds personal significance for me. Finally, the values represented by this acronym seamlessly align with my own principles and beliefs. Embracing these core values enables me to lead an authentic and fulfilling life, and guides me towards a path that is true to my essence.

The WINTER acronym also stands for:

Wellbeing: My approach to coaching and mentoring is holistic, aiming to ensure that all aspects of a client's life is valued.

Integrity: I operate with the highest level of integrity. This was borne out of me serving my country and adopting one of the military's values as my own, and I live by this daily.

Nurturing: I have learned to nurture myself, and this has taught me that no hurdle is insurmountable, so long as I have the right support and guidance. Every challenge can be overcome, and I am here to help my clients achieve this.

Trust: Positive outcomes are built on trust, so I am not afraid to be myself. I encourage people to build trust with me so I can help them be the best they can be.

Empathy: As a coach my role is not to judge my clients. I am simply another resource to help you become the best version of yourself that you can be.

Resilience: This is the cornerstone of both happiness and success. My life experience has taught me resilience, and I strive to help everyone I work with develop resilience across all areas.

In the journey of aligning with your authentic self, the next vital step is to cultivate self-awareness and to listen to your intuition while setting clear intentions. Embracing vulnerability and being open to personal growth and transformation are essential aspects of living authentically. Trusting the process of self-discovery guides your actions and empowers you to make decisions that resonate with your true essence, even if they challenge societal norms or expectations.

Your gut feelings and instincts offer valuable insights that can lead you towards choices aligned with your authentic values. For instance, prioritising a healthy lifestyle can be a significant intention, prompting you to focus on regular exercise, nourishing meals and self-care. Self-care encompasses nurturing your physical, emotional and mental wellbeing by engaging in activities that bring joy and rejuvenation, such as spending time with loved ones or pursuing creative endeavours.

Taking care of yourself enables you to show up authentically in both personal and professional spheres. Drawing from personal experience, I have learned the importance of not neglecting my intuition and self-care during stressful job roles, as it can adversely affect mental health and physical health. By consciously shaping the life I desire and aligning it with my authentic self, I have discovered clarity and inner peace, and this has led to significant improvements in both my physical and mental wellbeing.

In pursuit of personal growth and alignment with your authentic self, setting and maintaining boundaries is an essential aspect of the journey. Boundaries act as protective measures to safeguard your time, energy and resources, helping to prevent external demands and distractions from derailing you from your path. As you embark on this transformative journey, it is crucial to surround yourself with a supportive network of like-minded individuals who respect and encourage your boundaries.

My role as a coach is to guide you towards establishing clear and healthy boundaries. The first step is cultivating self-awareness. By exploring your values, priorities and personal limits, you gain deeper insights into what truly matters to you. This self-awareness will enable you to identify areas where boundaries are necessary and how they can be beneficial in maintaining a balanced and fulfilling life.

With the help of a coach or supportive network, you can define the boundaries for different aspects of your life, be it in your work, relationships or personal time. These boundaries act as guides to protect your wellbeing and prevent burnout. A coach should help you explore the intricacies of setting boundaries and addressing situations in which assertiveness and effective communication are required to establish and maintain these limits.

Throughout your journey, your coach should be able to help you recognise instances where your boundaries may be tested or violated. Identifying boundary violations can empower you to address such situations with confidence and to reinforce your boundaries with assertiveness and clarity. It is normal to face challenges in maintaining boundaries, but with regular coaching check-ins and support, you will learn to navigate these situations and strengthen your commitment to self-care.

Surrounding yourself with a supportive network will be instrumental in maintaining your boundaries. A coach will encourage you to seek out people who share your values and encourage your growth. Having people around you who respect and understand your boundaries will provide the encouragement and reinforcement needed to stay true to your authentic self.

As you progress on this journey, you will experience a profound transformation in how you navigate life's challenges and prioritise your wellbeing. By setting and maintaining boundaries, you create the space to pursue what truly matters to you, while safeguarding your energy and focus. The process of identifying and setting boundaries is an act of self-love and empowerment that will enable you to live authentically and to authentically embrace the life you desire.

By investing in yourself and taking courageous action, you will be able to identify and mitigate or harness your weaknesses. By taking action you will also be able to focus on your strengths. This is the key to unlocking your true potential and leading a fulfilling life.

Each of us possesses unique talents and abilities that set us apart, and harnessing them can boost our confidence, engagement and sense of fulfilment. Reflect on your strengths and contemplate how you can apply them, both personally and professionally. Embrace opportunities that align with your authentic self, even if they seem daunting at first. For example, if you have always dreamed of pursuing a creative career but hesitated due to fear or uncertainty, take a brave step forward by enrolling in art classes or starting a side project that nurtures your artistic passion.

In my own journey, I had a deep desire to help others, yet fear and the need for financial stability kept me from pursuing my dream for many years. However, with encouragement, I summoned the courage to focus on my strengths as a people-oriented person and undertook the transition from engineering work to developing my coaching practice. Despite taking this profound and important step, I continued to feel unfulfilled. It was through introspection and embracing my engineering expertise that I discovered a career opportunity that now allows me to share my knowledge and to teach and mentor the next generation of graduates and women in STEM. This alignment with my authentic self has brought unparalleled joy and fulfilment to my life. The positive energy I exude is palpable to those I teach, coach and mentor, and has resulted in me receiving nominations for Engineer of the Year and Mentor of the Year awards for three consecutive years.

Finally, practise self-reflection. Regularly taking time to reflect on your thoughts, feelings and actions can help you stay aligned with your authentic self. Consider journalling, meditating or engaging in other reflective practices that deepen your self-awareness and help you gain clarity on your values and goals. Aligning your actions with your authentic self is essential for living a fulfilling and meaningful life. It requires a willingness to be honest with yourself, to acknowledge your strengths and weaknesses, and to set clear boundaries that protect your time and energy. By focusing on your strengths, practising self-care, seeking support and practising self-reflection, you can cultivate trust in your intuition and start living authentically.

The role of accountability

Living authentically requires a strong sense of accountability, as it provides the necessary structure and support to help you stay true to your values and commitments. When you hold yourself accountable, you take ownership of your actions and decisions, empowering yourself to live intentionally and authentically. I have attended many motivational seminars and watched many TED talks. Whilst I cannot remember where I heard this, I had it written down in the front of my journal. I feel it to be sage advice about being authentic and accountable. "Be true to yourself. Be the best that you can be. When you make a mistake, learn from it, pick yourself up, and move on". Embracing this mindset, even in the face of challenges and mistakes, allows you to remain steadfast on your authentic path.

One effective way to keep yourself accountable is by finding an accountability partner or joining a support group that shares your values and goals. These connections offer guidance and encouragement to help you stay on track. Additionally, employing a goal-setting framework, like setting SMART goals, which emphasise Specific, Measurable, Achievable, Relevant and Time-bound objectives, can assist you in creating clear and actionable steps that align with your values and hold you accountable to your authentic self.

Accountability is a powerful tool for living authentically because it helps you stay committed to your goals and values, even when faced with challenges or obstacles. By finding an accountability partner or joining a support group, using a goal-setting framework and committing to acting towards your authentic self, you can create a life that feels true and fulfilling. Living authentically means aligning your thoughts, feelings and actions with your core values and beliefs. This is easier said than done, especially when external factors can sometimes influence our decisions and actions. However, it is possible to live authentically and be true to oneself.

CASE STUDY
Emily's accountability practice

Emily is a young professional who was struggling to find fulfilment in her job. She wanted to know my secret to vitality. Through our coaching sessions Emily revealed that she had always been interested in pursuing a career in the arts, but she felt like it was too risky to pursue that path, mainly due to pressure from her parents. After some soul-searching, Emily realised that living authentically meant pursuing her passions, even if it meant taking a leap of faith and going against her parents' wishes.

Over a six-month period, I worked with Emily to develop SMART goals to hold herself accountable. She wanted to take an art class once a week for three months. By focusing on small steps, Emily found a local art studio and signed up for a class, and committed to attending every week no matter how busy she was with work. As she was only being coached monthly, one of her SMART goals was to identify a friend who could be her accountability buddy. Emily encouraged a close friend who was also interested in art to commit with her so she could stay motivated and committed to her goal.

Over time, Emily's confidence grew as she honed her skills and discovered a renewed passion for art. Eventually, she made the brave decision to leave her job and pursue a full-time career in the arts. I am pleased to say that due to her talents, her fear of not living up to her parents' expectations were unfounded, as her parents admitted that all they wanted for her was to be happy and successful. Emily used to think the success her parents wanted for her was financial, but it turned out that they meant they wanted her to be successful by doing whatever made her happy. By aligning her actions with her authentic self and holding herself accountable to her goals, Emily was able to create a life that felt true to who she was and was able to overcome the fear of letting her parents down.

Final thoughts

Throughout this book, I have provided strategies and ideas to help you live a more authentic life. To wrap up, here is a summary of these ideas.

Set boundaries

It is important to set boundaries in our personal and professional lives to protect our energy and time. Saying "no" when necessary can be difficult, but it is essential if we are to maintain our mental and emotional wellbeing. By setting boundaries, you are taking control of your life and making choices that align with your values.

Practise self-care

Self-care is about taking care of your physical, emotional and mental health. It can be as simple as getting enough sleep, eating nutritious food or going for a walk. When we take care of ourselves, we are better able to show up authentically in all areas of our lives.

Honour your values

Understanding your core values is crucial in living authentically. When we act in ways that go against our values, we experience internal conflict and turmoil. By honouring your values, you are living in alignment with your authentic self.

Seek support

Living authentically can be challenging, and it is okay to ask for help. Surround yourself with people who support and encourage you to be yourself. Joining a support group or seeking guidance from a coach or therapist can also be helpful.

Embrace vulnerability

Being vulnerable can be scary, but it is essential in living authentically. When we open ourselves up to vulnerability, we allow ourselves to be seen and heard, which can be empowering. By embracing vulnerability, we can connect more deeply with ourselves and others, fostering genuine and meaningful relationships.

Take action

Living authentically requires action. It is not enough to just understand our values and beliefs; we must act on them. Take small steps towards living an authentic life, whether it is having a difficult conversation, pursuing a new hobby or making a career change. Remember, each step, no matter how small, brings you closer to your authentic self.

Celebrate progress

Acknowledge and celebrate your progress along the way. Recognise the courage it takes to live authentically and appreciate the growth you experience as you align your actions with your values. Celebrate your achievements, no matter how big or small, as they are a testament to your commitment to living authentically.

Practise self-compassion

Living authentically is a continuing journey, and there will be times when you stumble or face setbacks. Be kind to yourself during these moments. Practise self-compassion and remember that it is okay to make mistakes. Treat yourself with the same understanding and empathy you would offer to a close friend.

Be open to growth and change

Embrace the idea that growth and change are natural parts of living authentically. As you evolve and gain new insights about yourself, be open to adjusting your goals and values accordingly. Allow yourself the freedom to grow and change without judgement or limitation.

In conclusion, living authentically is about aligning your thoughts, actions and values with your true self. It requires courage, self-awareness and accountability. By setting boundaries, practising self-care, honouring your values, seeking support, embracing vulnerability, taking action, celebrating progress and practising self-compassion, you can create a life that feels true and fulfilling.

As you embark on your journey to living authentically, remember that it is okay to take things one step at a time. Each step, no matter how small, contributes to your growth and progress. Embrace the process, cherish your uniqueness and trust that by living authentically you will find a sense of purpose, fulfilment and joy that can only come from living life as your most genuine self.

So, take the first step today towards activating your authenticity. Embrace your fears, trust your intuition and honour your true self. You deserve to live a life that aligns with your values and purpose, and the world needs your authentic self to shine bright.

Further Reading

Adams, M. (2004), *Change Your Questions, Change Your Life*, Berrett-Koehler Publishers.

Annis, B. & Gray, J. (2013), *Work With Me*, Pitakus.

Baggini, J. & Macro, A. (2012), *The Shrink and the Sage: A Guide to Living*, Icon Books.

Brown, B. (2012), *Daring Greatly*, Penguin Random House.

Bishop, G. J. (2016), *Unf*ck Yourself*, Yellow Kite Publishing.

Dyer, W. W. (1977), *Pulling Your Own Strings*, Harper Collins.

—— (1991), *Your Sacred Self*, Harper Collins.

—— (2006), *Living an Inspired Life*, Hay House.

—— (2007), *Change Your Thoughts, Change Your Life*, Hay House.

—— (2009), *Excuses Begone*, Hay House.

Duckworth, A. (2017), *GRIT*, Penguin Random House.

Fields, J. (2021), *Sparked*, Harper Collins.

Fox, J. (2014), *The Game Changer*, Wiley.

Eurich, T (2017), *Insight*, Pan Macmillan.

Goleman, D. (1996), *Emotional Intelligence*, Bloomsbury.

—— (1998), *Working with Emotional Intelligence*, Bloomsbury.

Grant, A. (2021), *Think Again*, Penguin Random House.

Groover, R. J. (2011), *Powerful and Feminine*, Deep Pacific Press.

Hendricks, G. (2009), *The Big Leap*, Harper One.

Mackay, H. (2010), *What Makes Us Tick*, Hachette.

—— (2013), *The Good Life*, Pan Macmillan

—— (2020), *The Inner Self*, Pan Macmillan.

Medina, J. (2011), *Brain Rules*, Scribe.

Mercurio, Z. (2017), *The Invisible Leader*, Advantage.

O'Keefe, A. (2011), *Hardwired Humans*, Roundtable Press.

Rock, D. (2009), *Your Brain at Work*, Harper Business.

Sandberg, S. 2015), *Lean In: Women, Work and the Will to Lead*, Penguin Random House.

Simpson, N. (2015), *Live What You Love*, Harlequin.

Sinek, S. (2017), *Find Your Why*, Penguin Random House.

Winfrey, O. (2014), *What I Know For Sure*, Pan Macmillan.

Milton Keynes UK
Ingram Content Group UK Ltd.
UKHW051019201123
432909UK00013BA/388

9 780645 998009